HOW STORY WORKS

An elegant guide to the craft of storytelling

by Lani Diane Rich

Published by Chipperish Media
chipperish.com
lanidianerich.com

For permissions contact lani@chipperish.com

Cover by Lani Diane Rich.

ISBN: 9798785920682

Printed in the United States

First Edition

DEDICATION

For Dr. Kelly Jones

Kintsugi, baby.

Kintsugi.

TABLE OF CONTENTS

HOW THIS BOOK WORKS

If you picked up this book, maybe it's because you're feeling frustrated in your writing. Maybe you're curious about story craft, or you're stuck at a plot point you can't figure out how to resolve. Maybe it's a class text. Maybe, like me, you signed a contract for two books and you have no idea how you wrote the first one, let alone how you're going to do a second one. That's how I fell down the story craft rabbit hole and now, nearly two decades of study later, I'm finally ready to share with you everything I've learned in that time.

It's a lot. Buckle up, buttercup.

But first, a few things.

1. This is a book about story craft. The purpose of story craft is to get you out of your own way so that your magic can shine. There's a chapter later in this book called "Craft and Magic" where I explain these concepts in more detail, but for now, just know that this book gets you through the technical aspects of story craft so you can do what you came to storytelling to do: shine.

2. This is a deliberately short book. That is because so many of the instructions on writing out there are way more complicated than they have to be. *How Story Works* will show you just that: how story works. It's good that it's short; you'll need to reference it multiple times to really absorb it all. It's meant to work like *Elements of Style*, all beat up and smudged

on your bookshelf from how frequently you'll need to paw through it.

3. If you're looking to be a New York Times bestselling novelist or an Oscar-winning screenwriter, I can't do that for you. I will make your story better, but quality is not a predictor of commercial success. Quality means that if the lightning strike of success happens to hit you, you'll probably ride it out longer and with better reviews. But you can write a staggering piece of genius that no one ever buys, and you can write total crap that camps at the top of the bestseller list for ages. I have no control over that, and darling, neither do you. But if that's what you're here looking for, let me save you some money up front.

    a. Give a severe side-eye to anyone who makes those kinds of promises. They are promising something they cannot deliver.

Now that we've covered the fact that I'm *not* here to teach you your own magic and I'm *not* here to make you a best-selling novelist or an Oscar-winning screenwriter, let me tell you what I *am* gonna do.

I'm gonna define story for you, teach you basic narrative theory and how to apply it to your work, and give you the tools you need to get the job done. I'm going to make you a more effective storyteller, and I'm gonna help you get out of your own way so you can get the craft part done efficiently, and let your magic shine.

What happens after that is entirely up to you.

COURSE TEXTS

The following stories are used as examples in this book, and there may be some spoilers.

Movies

Disney's Snow White and the Seven Dwarfs

Dodgeball

Dr. Horrible's Sing Along Blog

French Kiss

Guardians of the Galaxy

His Girl Friday

Jaws 4: The Revenge

Megamind

Memento

Raiders of the Lost Ark

Roxanne

Tangled

The Fugitive

The Lord of the Rings

The Martian

Toy Story

Young Adult

Television Series

Buffy the Vampire Slayer

Game of Thrones

Moonlighting

Sherlock

The Good Place

The Office

Novels

Harry Potter series

The Handmaid's Tale

Wicked

1. ON STORY

It's the fall of 1989, my freshman year of college, and I hustle over to the local convenience store between classes to buy some gum. I'm standing in line behind some kid with a suitcase of beer in one hand and his ID in the other, and I glance at the ID.

'Cuz I'm just that kind of girl.

And it looks… well, weird. Now, I, as an 18-year-old young woman from a very small town who has very little experience of the big, wide world, am no expert on fake IDs, but I'm pretty sure this one had to be fake.

I mean, come on.

It's from Delaware.

I chuckle to myself and say a silent prayer for the future of this poor, dumb kid who has been taken in SO completely by such a stupid scam. Selling bad fakes, that's a time-honored American tradition, but come on… Delaware?

I mean, everyone knows Delaware isn't a state.

The line moves and I'm standing behind this guy, waging an internal war between minding my own damn business and giving the poor guy a heads up that he was swindled before he gets publicly humiliated. The shy part of me wins out. The line moves, it moves again, and finally, the guy puts his suitcase of beer down on the counter and hands the cashier dude his ID and I'm cringing as I wait and…

Dude sells him the beer.

He *sells* him the *beer.*

The fake ID guy trots on out with his beer, so… okay. I buy my gum in stunned silence and then go to class, but that night as all my friends are hanging out in the common room of our suite, I say, "Oh my god, you guys, I have got to tell you what happened today!"

And I proceed to tell the story, just the way that I'm telling you now, and when I get to the good part—his ID was from *Delaware*—there's nothing.

Blank stares.

Silence.

Crickets.

"Delaware," I say again, waiting for it to sink in. "Del-a-ware. It's not a state. It's a town. It's a river in Maryland."

And then they all bust out laughing and I'm standing there like, "What?"

So a friend of mine gets out the dictionary which has a map of the U.S. in it—this was in the pre-internet days when we still needed and carried around actual books—and shows me that not only is Delaware a state…

… it's the *first* state.

WHAT IS STORY?

What I just told you was a story, right? You recognized it. A series of events, a retelling… a story. It's like pornography; you know it when you see it, but even a Supreme Court justice is gonna have to pause to specifically *define* it. The reason for that isn't due to the complexity of what a story is; it's due to the ubiquity. Go ahead: Describe air.

See what I mean?

So, let's start out here by defining our terms, an important part of the process when learning anything. Now, my definition of some terms may vary a bit from the standard dictionary definitions; I'm defining these terms to suit our purposes here, because sometimes, the dictionary isn't quite specific enough.

My apologies to both Merriam and Webster; no offense, huge fan.

Let's start with **story**; what is story?

STORY:
A recounted event or series of events

That's it; very simple.[1] Story is a recounted event or series of events. Let's pause a moment here and pay attention to one word that we might skip over, but we shouldn't: recounted.

---

[1] It's deceptively simple, and specific, and that specificity may trip you up a few times before we're done here, so you might want to highlight it or write it down on a post-it or make a note in your notes app of choice or have it tattooed on your inner arm. You do you, punkin.

A story isn't the event or series of events themselves; a story is the recounting of those events. This is incredibly important; because in order for a story to be a story, it has to be told, and in being told, it will be edited. Random events throughout a day are just events until someone edits out the unimportant details and recounts the story with a specific meaning in mind, thus creating a narrative.

Let's expand on *that* a bit.

NARRATIVE:
The meaning evoked by a story

A story is the recounted series of events; narrative is the meaning evoked when those events are shaped to serve that meaning.

Now here's a thing; you're going to hear story and narrative used interchangeably. Hell, I might even do it, because I'm teaching you **storytelling**, and storytelling is where story and narrative combine.

STORYTELLING:
The art of building a story purposefully to serve a particular narrative

We recount a story in a particular way to evoke a particular meaning. Meaning is why we engage in fiction. When I talk about story in this book, I'm talking about a particular kind of story. One that evokes a specific and deliberate meaning. Everything we are learning about story here is specifically designed to help you express your narrative.

Have you ever bumped into someone you knew on the street and they started telling you all the things that happened to them that day? And you sat there, politely listening, thinking, "Jeez, Agnes. Get to the point, will you?"

Agnes has told you a story… a recounted series of events. But Agnes did not have a *purpose* to her story. She did not provide *narrative*.

So, we've covered recounted, now let's hit on our second important concept when talking about story and narrative: **meaning**.

MEANING:
The implied or explicit significance of a thing

Let's say that when you bump into Agnes on the street this time, she tells you about how she got up early because she had to rush to work for her big presentation but then some dumb and very big dog had shit a brick right next to her car door and she stepped in it. Like…. *really* stepped in it. So she throws her stuff into her car and runs to the back yard to grab the garden hose, but the garden hose was split and it sprayed water… and bits of dog poo… all over her, but then her colleague Eddie called and told her that the CEO's flight got rescheduled so Agnes's presentation was pushed to later in the day, thank god, and Agnes breathes a sigh of relief and goes inside to change her outfit *and* her shoes and fix her makeup, but then when she gets to work, she discovers nothing was ever rescheduled and the CEO left thinking Agnes just didn't show up and then Eddie said something under his breath about garden hoses that stuck with her, so when Agnes went home, she checked her garden hose and it hadn't split… it had been cleanly sliced.

And Eddie, she now recalls, told her once that he named his Newfoundland dog "Brick" because when it shits, it shits… well… bricks.

Wow. Now Agnes's story is actually interesting… because it has focus.

Because it has structure.

Because all the details contribute to one meaning... that Eddie is a sneaky little snake.

That's meaning.

That's *narrative*.

This is a big deal, by the way, the editorial nature of recounting, the choosing of what to leave in and what to leave out, what matters and what does not. Agnes may have also had a vanilla latte that morning. She might have been listening to a *Buffy the Vampire Slayer* podcast on her headphones when she stepped in the dog poo. But she doesn't tell you that, because none of that has anything to do with Eddie, who is the focus of this story.

Agnes recounted the story in such a way as to evoke meaning; Agnes gave you narrative, and narrative is the most essential part of the story.

A story, whether true or fictional, does not gain narrative until someone has gone in and monkeyed with the details to make sure that everything included contributes toward an intended meaning.

Let's revisit these core concepts:

STORY:
A recounted event or series of events

NARRATIVE:
The meaning evoked by a story

STORYTELLING:
The art of building a story purposefully to serve a particular narrative

The Delaware Story, as it has been called by me and my friends for decades now, is a funny story because it is recounted in such a way that every chosen detail, from the suitcase of beer that required the kid to hold his ID where I could see it to what I thought Delaware was ("It's a town, a river in Maryland.") to the dictionary my friend hauled out to show me my error, contributes to the overall meaning of the story. Both explicit and implied, the meaning of this story is that the mocker can become the mocked all too easily, and let's not get too full of ourselves, shall we?

You can have a series of events, but if in the end that series of events is random, not building up into something bigger and more significant than the mere sum of its parts, it won't be as powerful. Ramping up that narrative power requires the editorial process in recounting, in order to produce meaning.

No editing, no meaning.

No meaning, no narrative.

As we will discuss in the chapters on structure, story meaning is derived from how the world of the story changes. But what's important there is not just *how* the world has changed, but *why* it changed.

We, as humans, are always on a desperate search for the why. It wasn't enough to see the sun come up every morning; we had to know *why*. Everything is about *the why*.

And the why is the reason why story is the most powerful force on earth, I'm not even joking with you.

Let me show you what I'm talking about. Let's say, I have a bicycle and one day, I accidentally ride it into the side of my house and get a scratch on it. Okay. I'm not very coordinated. It happens. It goes to the shop.

That's a story.

Another scenario: let's say I go out in the morning ready for my ride and I notice a scratch on my bike that definitely wasn't there the night before. And let's say I also happen to have a mean-spirited neighbor who hates my barking dog, and I remember seeing that very neighbor walking by my house last night with her keys in her hand…

That's a story *with narrative*. My vengeful neighbor clearly scratched my bike in a passive aggressive attempt to get back at me for having a barky dog.

In both scenarios, the physical reality is the same. My bike is scratched, and I have to take it in for repairs. But in one story, I'm just a klutz and stuff happens.

In the other, I'm the victim of a crime against bikes.

And *dogs*.

Same physical reality. Same basic events. Two totally different narratives.

Now, is the story about my neighbor actually true? It doesn't matter. I *believe* it's true. I created a story, and in my reality, the meaning behind that story, the *narrative*, is absolutely true.

That story's narrative has just molded reality for me.

It changed my world.

So, when I say that story is the most powerful force on earth—and I will say that, a lot—I'm not messing around. Story, when infused with a strong narrative, literally holds the power of life and death.

Wars are waged based on the story of who is the hero, and who is the villain. People die.

You, your life, your existence on this planet, is the result of a story your parents told each other. It could be the story of soul mates, or the casual one-night stand, but trust me, there was a story there, and that's why you're here.

Death.

Life.

Story.

This is the beginning of this wild ride, learning about narrative theory and talking about everything that story touches… which is *everything*.

Ready for another reality about the power of story that tends to knock writers off their barstools?

It's not you, as the storyteller, who decides what a story means.

It's the reader.

READER:
Any person who derives meaning from any story, regardless of form

For our purposes here, the **reader** is the person who "reads" the story as recounted, and it doesn't matter if the form is a novel, a movie, a video game, or a cartoon scrawled on a bar napkin.

Don't get caught up on form, by the way. We're drilling down to the essential basics of storytelling, and these principles can be universally applied. No one form is superior to any other: song lyrics, novels, short films, comedy routines. The value of a story is not found in form, and snobbery hurts the snob more than anyone else, so if you've got any remnants of form snobbery wafting around in that brilliant head of yours, sweep it out now. It's nonsense and it'll just get in your way.

Back to this business with the reader deciding what something means, not the storyteller.

As a storyteller, you may recount your series of events to serve a particular narrative, but in the end, you don't decide what it means. Five people may read it and come away with five different experiences, deriving five different meanings from your work, some or none of which may be what you intended, and all of which are equally valid to *their* experience.

Well, that sounds like total chaos, you might think, and you'd be right.

But it's okay. It's just how it is. A signal goes out, but it doesn't mean anything until it's received. And once it's received, it's not really your business as the storyteller how it's received. You can't control that. You can only control what you send out.

Let's return to my Delaware story. I've told you the meaning; a young girl's hubris brings her down. I formed the narrative specifically to get that point across, and probably, most of you received the message I sent out; a funny story, presented without ego and no small amount of self-deprecation, about how I was an idiot and it's no big deal.

But some of you might have picked up a tale about the ultimate failure of our public school system; or the hesitancy of a young girl to speak up in a situation where she might be wrong, and the role of the patriarchy in that hesitancy; or the tendency toward self-deprecation in women. If you picked up any of those narratives, or maybe something else entirely, what you picked up was legit. If you saw it, it was there. It may not be what I intended, but if a reader sees it, it's there, and to my storytellers, my writers, my recounters, my message is this:

Deal with it.

It is what it is and it's the cost of admission to wield the chaotic beauty that is storytelling.

And I, for one, wouldn't have it any other way. That said, the stronger your narrative game, the greater the chance that the reader will pick up *exactly* what you intend. Understand, I'm not promising that with strong narrative game a reader will *never* see something you didn't intend; the beauty of art is that it belongs to both the artist and the audience. I'm just saying that'll happen less often.

Before we move on, let's talk a little bit about where the meaning, the significance, of a story comes from.

Meaning is derived from *change*. We can only tell what a story means when we see how the world, or character, has changed because of what has happened.

Let's go back to basic high school chemistry, a class in which I deeply disappointed my teacher, Mr. Dietrich, by almost burning my lab partner's eyebrows off with what I to this day purport to be a criminally faulty Bunsen burner. But I did retain one thing; until you can observe a change, you can't figure out what an experiment means. In chemistry class, I could combine chemical A and chemical B, but if nothing changed, I couldn't be sure what, if anything, had happened.

But if I put chemical A with chemical C, and the solution turned blue, then I had something to work with; a change was affected, and I could observe that change and try to figure out what it means.

Same with story.

We take a character and we put them through hell and see what changes.

That's one of your jobs as a writer, by the way; just torment your characters from start to finish. Force them into uncomfortable situations where they have to face their darkest demons and make impossible choices in order to win in a battle that is life and death to them, and then... see what happens.

How does that character change? How does the story world change?

That can be confusing sometimes, because the "story world" is not just the external reality of the characters in your story. A story world also includes the internal world of your characters. You can have a story in which the external world doesn't change much at all, but if the internal perspective of your protagonist significantly shifts, you've got meaning. This is often referred to as a character arc; when a character starts out in one mental or emotional place, and transitions into another as a result of the events of the story.

And while we're here, same thing for story arc; it's basically the change that happens to the world as your story moves from one set of conditions into another at the end.

How Middle Earth and the characters in it change in *The Lord of the Rings* is the story arc. What happens to an individual character is the character arc, and that's where your gold is mined. As readers, our emotional investment is with the characters, like Frodo and Sam, our plucky heroes. Sam leaves the Shire an innocent and he returns more worldly and experienced, but his essential innocence, his innate goodness, his ability to connect to the world he fought so hard to save, remains untouched.

Frodo, however, is so changed by his experience of trying to save the Shire that he can no longer live there; he must go to the grey lands with the elves and live out his existence as something different from what he was when the story began.

And what does that mean? Is this a story about looking into the abyss which looks back into you? Did Frodo wear the ring too much, for too long, such that it changed him so fundamentally that he would never be the same? Does it mean that Sam was a purer soul than Frodo because he was able to go to the dark places, to carry the ring, and yet return home still fundamentally himself?

I don't know.

You're the reader.

You decide.

THE DIFFERENCE BETWEEN STORY AND FORM

Okay, what do we have so far?

Story is a recounted event or series of events; narrative is the meaning evoked by a story; and storytelling is the art of building a story purposefully to serve a particular narrative.

So, what is, let's say, your novel? Is it a story? A narrative?

It's neither. Your novel is the **form** in which you choose to deliver your story, and it's important to make that distinction.

For a writer to make the most of the tools at their disposal, they need to know the purpose of each. Form is the medium through which an artist works. As a writer, you can use a form to express a story, but they are distinct things.

FORM:
The medium through which an artist works

When I'm talking about form, I'm talking about novels, films, poetry; an episode of television, a thirty-second radio ad, a fictionalized podcast. Form is the thing you are creating; story is something you may choose to express through that form, but it is *not* the form itself.

Now, I'm a novelist, right? I tell my stories in a particular form—books. Yet I teach screenwriting, and I teach creators working in advertising, public relations, and journalism how to use storytelling in their chosen fields. I use the same basic toolset to critique stories whether they come from books, movies, television, video games, whatever. Many writing books mix story and form together; they'll tell you how to write a novel, or a screenplay, or a comic book. There are different tools associated with any particular form, but the basic building blocks of narrative—what I'm teaching you in this book—are transcendent of form.

Form is simply the delivery mechanism for the story; it is not the story itself. It's the novel, the movie, the TV show, the video game. All of these forms are capable of delivering story, but may not be primarily concerned with delivering a story built with *strong* narrative. Some might be open-ended, ambiguous, more concerned with the randomness of verisimilitude than the dogged editorial bent of narrative.

In short, just because a particular form *can* deliver a strong and clearly built narrative, doesn't mean it always *does*.

Let's say a director of a film is very interested in the visual and audio qualities of the movie. They're focused on the art of the form, paying careful attention to making it as richly beautiful as it can be, frame by frame. This doesn't preclude the film from also having a strong story, but narrative craft is not going to be the primary focus. Terrence Malick is a good example of this kind of director. Controlling the narrative doesn't appear, to me, to be Malick's priority; he seems

18

primarily concerned with creating beautiful art within the form of film. There's story there—there's a recounted series of events—but it doesn't necessarily concern itself with delivering a strongly constructed narrative.

And this is true of every form—books, video games, television commercials, whatever. They *can* carry a constructed narrative, but they don't *have* to, and the degree to which they evoke meaning can also vary.

And that's okay. Some storytellers want the reader to carry more of the responsibility for deciding what a particular piece of art means. Some creators *want* the locus of meaning to be inside the reader; they provide some clues, but the reader decides how those clues go together to evoke a particular meaning. With those works of art, you're going to find a much broader range of ascribed meanings from the readers.

And you know what? There is nothing wrong with that. What I'm teaching in this book is for the creators who want to direct the narrative that emerges in their work. Do not take that to mean that I believe one style of artistic expression is superior to the other. My theory just speaks to the kind of story where the locus of meaning lies mostly with the creator. This allows your reader to be carried more through the story, opening up some space for one of the most powerful delights of engaging with fiction: **narrative transport**.

NARRATIVE TRANSPORT:
When a reader's current reality fades away, and the reader lives for a time within the reality of the story

I have yet to meet a reader who hasn't had the experience of narrative transport, those moments when you're reading something and the world around you fades away while you experience the story as though it is *actual* reality.

You stroll the halls of Pemberley with Darcy and Elizabeth. You sneak into a teacher's private rooms with Harry, Ron, and Hermione at Hogwarts. You stand in the fiery heart of Mount Doom as Gollum meets his tragic end. And when a text pings on your phone or there's a knock on the door in the real world, you have a moment of vertigo as you are pulled out of the story world and back into the regular world.

That's narrative transport, and it is the ultimate magic of storytelling. That is what this book will help you create for your reader, if that's what you want to do with your work. The more well-crafted the story you tell… the more skillfully you build meaning from recounting those events… the better you can provide narrative transport for your reader.

So, that's the goal of this book; to teach you how to do that. But let me be clear; artists who don't do that are no lesser for it. That's an artist who is more about the form, and that kind of artist can create beautiful, engaging, evocative, transformative art. It's just not, primarily, about expressing a deeply constructed narrative. Having a clear understanding of the difference among story, narrative, and form will help you become an effective storyteller while utilizing the strengths of your chosen form. While typically it's the art house film or literary novel that tends to leave narrative more to the reader, and genre fiction that tends to control a tighter narrative, any form and any story can find itself at different places on this spectrum, and they are all equally valuable artistic expressions.[2]

In this book, I'm talking about the times where story steps into the driver's seat and directs the form toward the destination, the transport, the experience. Story can ride in a movie or a novel or a

---

[2] Yes, I just said genre is every bit as valuable artistically as literary fiction. Fight me.

television commercial or a painting. Story will take over any delivery mechanism if the creator makes it a priority.

HOW STORY WORKS: THEORY & METHOD

In the coming chapters, we're going to dive deep into the *How Story Works* method, but first, I'm going to give you a quick summary of what we've already covered, and what's to come. You're gonna want to bookmark, tag, or dog-ear this page so if you have a moment when you're like, "What? Where? How? Why?" at a later part of the book, you can come back here and get your grounding.

Understand that this theory is simple, but it will take a long time to master. You will want to come back and review material regularly as you engage with fictional stories, and as you write your own. You will not read this book in one day and never need it again. Everything you learn here requires that you make a continual practice of working with the principles of craft that you will find here.

HOW STORY WORKS: THEORY

o   A **story** is a is a recounted event, or series of events. Narrative is the meaning evoked by a story. Storytelling is the art of building a story purposefully to serve a particular narrative.

o   Stories are powerful because of their **meaning**. We can only tell what a story means when we see how the world, or character, has **changed** because of what has happened.

o **Magic** is the artistic imprint of a creator on a work they've created. It's what you, as a writer, care about. It's why you want to tell a story, and why readers want to read it. It's what it all means. Magic is the part of you that nestles into your stories and gives them life. Your magic is different from everyone else's magic, and it's why two people can write a story with the exact same story beats and end up with wildly different stories. Your magic is your creative fingerprint.

o **Craft** is the set of principles that guide storytelling. Craft exists to make a creator's magic more accessible to the reader.

o A well-crafted story provides **narrative transport** for the reader. Narrative transport is the experience in which a reader's consciousness leaves their own reality for a while and exists within the reality of the story.

o **Form** is the delivery mechanism for the story; it is not the story itself. It's the novel, the movie, the TV show, the video game.

o Ultimately, the meaning of a story is derived by the **reader**, based on how and why the story world changes.

o The writer's job is to **change the world**. How the world of the story changes, be it the external world or the internal world of the main character, will define what a story means.

HOW STORY WORKS: METHOD

A story, whether true or fictional, does not gain power without narrative craft. The *How Story Works* method is based on principles of **conflict**, **structure** and **character** that will help you build stronger, more effective stories capable of providing narrative transport for your reader. These are stories crafted to deliver meaning (narrative) and allow your magic to shine.

The *How Story Works* method will teach you how to:

- lock your protagonist and antagonist in a **central narrative conflict;**

- **structure** your story to start, escalate, and end that central narrative conflict and then show how the world has changed;

- and create compelling **characters** whose goals drive the story.

In each of the following chapters, you will find tools that will help you apply the *How Story Works* method.

But before we get to the nuts and bolts of deeply constructed storytelling, we're going to need to understand a bit more about craft, and the reason why craft exists: to support magic.

2. CRAFT AND MAGIC

What I'm teaching you in this book is craft, which I will define specifically for our purpose of storytelling.

CRAFT:
The set of principles that guide storytelling

Craft is the structure and the character building and the conflict that keeps everything in the air. And that's all important. Clearly, I think so, as I've dedicated almost two decades of my life to understanding it so I could teach it to you.

But it's not the whole game.

It's not even *most* of the game.

Magic is the game, and craft lives in service to magic.

MAGIC:
The artistic imprint of a creator on their work

What is magic? It's like spirituality; it can be hard to describe, but you know it when you feel it. In the simplest terms, magic is that part of you that nestles into your stories and gives them life. Magic is how you see the universe. What you believe to be true. Magic is how you use a string of lies to tell the truth, and magic is what you believe that truth to be.

Magic is your voice, your sense of humor, your philosophical perspective, your take on right and wrong. Magic is what delights you, what scares you, what excites you, what breaks your heart.

It's what you care about, and it's what your readers care about.

It's what it all means.

And it's why the craft exists, to make your magic come through loud and clear.

ALIGNMENT

Some writers are aligned toward craft, and some are aligned toward magic.

For magic-aligned writers, craft is the boring part. In order for the play in their head to go on, a stage needs to be built, but they are not interested in the stage. Craft is predictable and boring. It's trade work. It's union dues. It's drudgery.

Magic-aligned writers want to get right to the magic, and so they say, "If magic is the good stuff, the important part, why do I have to bother with all this craft, building the stage to code or whatever? That's not *fun*."

I'd argue that it can be fun, that it indeed *is* fun, but it's also hard work, and it doesn't come naturally to everyone. For some writers, their very nature resists it. Even for craft-aligned writers, who absolutely love having something to put their backs up against when dealing with the terrifying *everything* that is creativity, it's a lot of work.

Believe it or not, I'm a magic-aligned writer. I have never really enjoyed the craft part. That's why, when I sold a two-book contract to Warner Books in 2003 off a book I wrote entirely fueled by magic and I had no idea how story actually worked, I dedicated myself to learning how it worked.

And that's how we got here.

But back to the craft-aligned writers. For them, craft is the whole game. It's rules, it's reason, it's a thing they can rationally understand when they're scared or panicked. Magic has nothing to do with rationality or reason, and it's terrifying for some writers. Craft is not vulnerable; it's math. You can show your work and see where you went wrong and know what needs fixing. If you focus on craft, there's a plan. If it's broken, you can just go back to the blueprint and fix it.

Magic is vulnerability; not your character's, but *yours*. Magic reveals who you are, what you think, how you see the world, and here's the terrifying part: Some people *might not like it.*

Oh god. If magic is me, and they don't like my magic, then they don't like me. That's a panic attack on a plate, right there.

That said, I would argue that if you're doing your magic right, some people shouldn't like it. If everyone likes what you do, chances are, it's not genuine, brave, or interesting. Everyone might like that kind of work enough, but few will love it, and *very* few will be passionate about it. Personally, I'd rather have some people be passionate about what I do, while others don't get it or even actively dislike it, than do stuff that never takes goes near the territory of messy or brave.

Messy and brave is where the good work, the bold work, the interesting work happens. And if we're not in the game to be interesting, then we're just passing time, waiting for death. I mean, not to be overly dramatic but… right?

Also, it's not a bad thing to be scared when you're doing creative work. Just do as Elizabeth Gilbert says in her book *Big Magic*; allow fear to come with you on this journey. To be honest, you can hardly prevent it from coming along. It will throw itself through the passenger side window if you try to peel out of the driveway without it. Just make sure it's in the back seat with a coloring book and crayons. You do *not* want to let fear drive the car. It will take you straight to the safe, boring places, and no one learns anything there.

Wherever you fall on the spectrum of magic-aligned to craft-aligned, it doesn't matter. One is not better than the other; they're just different. You're fine right where you are. You will always look somewhere else on the spectrum and think you might be a better writer over there, but it's not true. You are exactly where you are supposed to be.

That doesn't mean that if you're craft-aligned, you don't need to engage with magic. Or, that if you're magic-aligned, you can get along without craft. It just means that there's nothing wrong with you where you are. You'll still have to limber up and reach outside of your comfort zone to pull in the part of your story that comes from the space you are less aligned with.

But it's important that you understand why craft, what I will teach you in this book, matters. Yes, it exists in service to magic, but that doesn't make craft any less important. Is Fred Astaire any less important than Ginger Rogers? No.

They're different. They work together. And together, they're a miracle.

Think of it like a performance. Magic is the main act, but if it doesn't have a stage to dance upon, the only people who will see it and understand what it's doing will be in the front. And that's great, but it screws over the rest of your audience that would also like to enjoy the show but can't because no one considered making the performance accessible to them when designing the experience.

Imagine being at a show without a stage, in a space where the performance is level with the floor and the seats don't rise up on an incline to give everyone equal access. There's also no acoustics, so you can only hear every couple of words of the performance, but the person crunching potato chips next to you is loud and clear.

Do you want to be in that audience? Knowing this amazing show is happening, but you don't have access to it? No. You're gonna leave that show a few minutes in. Because if you don't have access to what's happening, then you might as well get the grocery shopping done, right?

Conversely, do you, as an audience member, want to be in a theater where the stage is beautifully crafted, could hold up a whole line of stomping elephants, and all the seats rise on a perfect incline, but no one is *doing* anything? The company of players come out and they all point at the stage and say, "Will you look at that craftsmanship?" and you're like, "Great. So what?" You're leaving that theater, too, probably quicker than the one with the great performance you can't see or hear.

This is what the *How Story Works* method is about. I'm teaching you how to build the stage so that you can make your dance visible, accessible, and captivating to the largest audience possible.

You might be asking yourself, "If craft is in service to magic and magic is the most important thing, why aren't you teaching me that?"

And the answer is… that's not what we're here to do right now. Your magic is yours; it is individual to you, and no one can really teach it to you, they can only teach you where to look for it, and how. To help you gain access to your own magic, I recommend Elizabeth Gilbert's book *Big Magic* and Neil Gaiman's Masterclass, *The Art of Storytelling*; I think they do some of the best work in accessing and understanding magic that I've ever seen.

But craft? Now that, I can teach you.

And that's what we're going to do next.

3. NARRATIVE PRINCIPLES

In his seminal book on screenwriting, *Story*, Robert McKee opens by saying, "Story is about principles, not rules," and I agree. Rules are strict and inflexible, but story is malleable and changeable and surprising. That's part of its beauty. That said, there's a difference between taking a creative path toward building an effective story and deciding that as a creative, you don't need to understand the craft of your art. If you want to be really good at what you do, you need to learn the craft.

The narrative theory I'm going to teach you in this book is based on principles that will help you build stronger, more effective stories capable of providing narrative transport for your reader, but the wonderful thing about principles is that they are inherently flexible. Once you understand them, you can mold them into the shapes that best meet the needs of your story. There's a quote, commonly attributed to Picasso, that hits this idea on the money: "Learn the rules like a pro, so you can break them like an artist."[3]

---

[3] Yeah, yeah, I know. Picasso was a misogynistic turd. He was wrong about women. He was right about rules. Understanding a person's brilliance and complexity and brokenness as pieces of a total package will help you in writing character. Huh? Did I just use Picasso-sourced indignation as an inroad into talking about character? Hell, yeah, I did. And you're the only one who knows, because you're the only one who read the damn footnote. Good on you.

For example, when I talk about character in detail later in this book, I will tell you that a strong protagonist has three qualities:

They are our POV (Point of View) character;

Their pursuit of their goal provides the motive force for the story; and

They have the most at stake if they fail to achieve that goal.

But in the movie *Dodgeball* we have a protagonist in Peter LeFleur who doesn't meet all these requirements. He is definitely the character whose perspective we are in for most of the story, so we're good there. He does have a lot at stake—if he fails to get the money to save his gym, Average Joe's, he loses his livelihood—but, in the beginning especially, he doesn't seem to care that much if he does lose it, which makes his pursuit of his goal a little weak because he's not really pushing to play in the dodgeball tournament.

So, by my own theory, *Dodgeball* should be a weak story, right?

Not necessarily, and here's why: *Dodgeball* has a group protagonist that shores up the structural failings in the main protagonist. While Peter LeFleur doesn't seem to care much about the possibility of losing Average Joe's or playing in the dodgeball tournament, his friends—Justin, Dwight, Gordon, Owen, Kate, and Steve the Pirate—do care, and he cares about them. They provide the motive force necessary to move the story forward where he fails to be emotionally invested, at least in the beginning. These characters, with their shared goal in conflict with the antagonist's goal, can function as a group protagonist because, while it's not their gym, Average Joe's means a lot to them, and they mean a lot to Peter, so they can push him forward until he grows enough as a human to care.

And caring is key.

Peter's character arc is that he goes from being someone so afraid of failure that he literally can't care, to someone who finally finds the courage to let things matter to him. We need protagonists to care; that's what fuels the central narrative conflict. Just trust me for now; the central narrative conflict matters, and for it to work, our protagonist must care deeply about the goal they are pursuing.

A strong protagonist is one whose **POV we are in**, whose **pursuit of a goal provides the motive force for the story**, and who **has the most at stake if they lose the fight**. If we have a group protagonist, then as long as we have all of these qualities covered among the group, the story will hold up. *Dodgeball* functions because it meets the qualifications of a protagonist through another avenue.

And *that* is the difference between rules and principles; principles have flexibility built in, whereas rules are intransigent. A writer who follows the rules blindly might see a problem like this in their main character and change the character. A writer who understands the principle might find another way. Both are adhering to the principles of narrative theory, and for both, their protagonists will function in the story. Which way you choose to go is up to you.

And it's okay.

I'm not dogging rules. They exist for a reason; to make doing something easier, and writing is hard enough. Also, some writers find rules comforting, and that doesn't make them formulaic writers. It makes them writers who know themselves and know what they need, and good for them.

There's a real and tangible benefit to writing by the rules: if you know you have something you can put your back up against—a protagonist must be x, y, and z—it can relieve the Creator's Vertigo[4] a bit. So, if

---

[4] Creator's Vertigo: The sensation that you're in way over your head and have no idea how in the hell you're going to make this work and *why* did you decide to write anyway when you could have baked bread or done some gardening, things that come with rules and directions? Pardon me while I over-identify.

you're one of those writers who needs hard and fast rules to which you can anchor your creative boat, then by all means work with these principles **as though they are rules**.

But if you're a writer who tends to feel restricted and resentful with rules in play, then work with these principles as though they are principles. Which they are. If you can find another way to do things while still building a strong narrative story, then go for it.

The narrative theory in this book is customizable to any writer's process.

My narrative theory has three major pillars—**conflict**, **structure,** and **character**—but they are intimately intertwined. Characters are great, but without conflict and structure, they're just people sitting around. Meanwhile, conflict cannot exist without character, and structure cannot exist without characters in conflict. While the framework itself is deceptively simple, mastering it can take a while, specifically *because* these are principles, not rules. Learning rules is easy; do this, then this, and Bob's your uncle. But when you learn principles, you need to learn not only the principles, but why they exist, so when you break them, you can be sure your craft work is still serving the needs of your narrative. A story may break the rules, and still work. When you see that happening out in the wild while reading a story, take some time and think about *how* it works; you'll find the *ends* of a principle ("a protagonist must care about their conflict") matched with an unexpected *means* of getting there.

Look, ride in a car or on a donkey; what's important is that you get where you're going.

But hands down, the best way to master your understanding of how story works is to engage with story critically and do your own analysis as you go. Watch your favorite film and ask yourself; who is the protagonist? How well do they function as a protagonist? Who is the antagonist? What is the central narrative conflict? How does it inform the structure? When you're analyzing stories on your own, I highly recommend finding a partner, someone who is smart and cares about stories, to talk about the stories with. There is no better intellectual whetting stone than a smart friend.

Before we get deep into the weeds, I want to briefly explain to you what we're going to be talking about when it comes to the principles of the *How Story Works* narrative theory.

NARRATIVE THEORY

My narrative theory takes cues from work that people have been doing with story since the days of Aristotle. It includes many common concepts (such as antagonists and protagonists, acts, conflict, etc.) and it incorporates ideas I developed myself because I couldn't find a source for what I was looking for.

But what makes my theory awesome is this; it works independent of form, which means that whether you're writing a screenplay or a novel, or laying out the questlines in a video game, this theory will work for you.

It is comprised of three basic categories: Conflict, structure, and character.

In my classes, I use the metaphor of a train; if your story is a train, **conflict** is the fuel, **structure** is the tracks, and **character** is the passenger, with a specific and important destination in mind. These elements work together to get us to the destination: the meaning.

CONFLICT

Conflict is the fuel that keeps the story moving. Your protagonist, in pursuit of a goal, is blocked by an antagonist, in pursuit of a mutually exclusive goal. This locked conflict will keep these two forces pushing against each other through the run of the story. It also defines the structure of the story, because the story starts when the conflict starts, escalates as the conflict escalates, and ends when the conflict is decided and resolves into a changed world.

Sometimes, conflict can be confusing, because in any story, you might have a number of conflicts going on: between your antagonist and protagonist, or between other characters in subplots. You'll have conflicts that last for a scene, and conflicts that run through the whole story. You'll have conflicts that come down to philosophical disagreements or personality clashes between your characters, and conflicts that are based on two people with active goals that are in opposition.

But only one conflict—the **central narrative conflict**—will structure the story from beginning to end. Your central narrative conflict is defined by the mutually exclusive goals between your protagonist and your antagonist, and that is the conflict that will be the base of your story structure.

STRUCTURE

Once again, from the top: A story is a recounted event, or series of events. Narrative is the meaning evoked by a story, and storytelling is the art of building a story purposefully to serve a particular narrative. In order to build a story toward that purposeful end, creating meaning, we need to understand structure.

If you've been in the writing game for any amount of time, you've probably heard about some standard story structures out there. There's the Hollywood Formula, Save the Cat, the Hero's Journey, and many, many more. You can follow these structures, and they may work for you depending on what form you're working in, but you don't *have* to follow any of them, as long as you use this basic sourdough starter of structure:

1. The story **starts** when the central narrative conflict launches;

2. The story **escalates** as the central narrative conflict gets worse;

3. The story **ends** when the winner of central narrative conflict is decided;

4. The story is given **meaning** during the resolution, when you show how the events of the story have **changed the world**.

Start
Escalate
End
Change

If you like, commit this to memory as **SEE Change**. That's it; that is the entire base of story structure, right there. The structure is expandable depending on how many *escalations*—scenes that intensify the central narrative conflict—you add to your story between launching the central narrative conflict and ending it.

We will be going over this in much more detail as we move through this book, but this four-point principle of structure (SEE Change) is what you should always go back to. As long as you **start the conflict, escalate the conflict, end the conflict, and change the world**, you've got a structure that will work.[5]

------

[5] Note that as we move through this book , when I'm talking about SEE Change structure, I'm always talking about the central narrative conflict, but I will refer to it as "the conflict" as shorthand.

CHARACTER

Character is the most important part of your story, because without character, there *is* no story. After all, your entire conflict and structure is based on characters in conflict, so without them, you got nothing.

Every story requires at least one character and has at least two character roles:

The **protagonist**—from the Greek *pro* for first and *agon,* struggle or contest, so first in the contest—is the character whose pursuit of a goal is keeping the conflict alive.

The **antagonist**—*ant*, against, the opposing force in *agon*, struggle or contest—is the character whose pursuit of a mutually exclusive goal blocks the protagonist from achieving their goal.

In an internal conflict story, you can do the entire thing with one character, a protagonist who is also their own antagonist; a protagonist who wants two things that are in direct conflict. But the minimum for a story is one character, two roles.

The protagonist has a lot of weight to carry. Readers ride through the story on the back of your protagonist, and if you want them to experience narrative transport on that ride, you need your protagonist to be compelling.

Note that I did not say *likeable.* Forget likeable; anyone who tells you your protagonist needs to be more likeable is either dead wrong, or really means that the protagonist needs to be more *compelling.* We'll get into this idea more in the chapter on character, but I want to make that distinction because it's important, especially for writers who write female characters and are constantly being told to make them more likeable.

That's nonsense, sexist shenanigans. Shake the likeability monkey off your back now.

I use a concept I've developed called the **character triangle**, which encourages you to think consciously about the strengths, weaknesses and—most importantly—*vulnerabilities* of your characters. Most often, character problems stem from writers who don't think these elements of character through with enough clarity. Working through your characters with the character triangle will help you build strong characters that readers want to travel with.

These three areas of narrative theory—conflict, structure, and character—are the basic building blocks of a strong story.

All right. You're all prepped and ready to go.

Let's get into the weeds.

4. CONFLICT

Conflict is the fuel that keeps your story moving. Since how you build your characters depends on understanding the roles they play in the conflict, and the story structure is built as an escalation of conflict, it's probably best to start with conflict.

So… what is conflict?

CONFLICT:
A struggle between two opposing forces

You know what story is (a recounted event, or series of events) and you know what narrative is (the meaning evoked by a story), and you know that we derive a narrative's meaning from what has changed because of the events of that story.

So where does that change come from?

Simply put: Change comes from conflict.

Let's visit with the father of narrative theory, Isaac Newton.

Okay, maybe he didn't *know* he was contributing to narrative theory at the time, but he was. Newton's law that an object at rest will remain at rest until acted on by an unbalanced force is pretty relevant to narrative theory because, let's face it… story is about people, and people don't change unless they're acted on by some frickin' unbalanced forces.

In other words, people don't change unless they *have* to.

Since you're relying on change to give your story meaning, you're going to need a force in there applying pressure, pushing your characters and their world toward that change.

You're going to need *conflict*.

So, to alter Newton's Law to our own purposes, a character or situation will remain the same unless a force (conflict) acts upon them, giving them no choice but to change.

You figure out a story's meaning by seeing what has changed, and you get change through conflict. Simple right?

Yes.

And no.

Of course.

Because here's the thing; there are different kinds of conflict, some of which will fuel your story, and some of which won't. Much like you don't want to put diesel fuel into a car that takes unleaded, you also need to be sure that you're filling your story with the right kind of conflict.

You need *narrative* conflict.

NARRATIVE CONFLICT VS. MUNDANE CONFLICT

Conflict is a struggle between two opposing forces. Simple. Get two people disagreeing on something and you've got conflict.

What you don't necessarily have, however, is conflict that can keep a story in the air for the entire run, conflict that forces change, which in turn creates meaning.

What you don't necessarily have is *narrative* conflict.

NARRATIVE CONFLICT:
A goal-based conflict between a protagonist with a goal and an antagonist with a mutually exclusive goal

Narrative conflict is a conflict between a protagonist and an antagonist in pursuit of mutually exclusive goals. By mutually exclusive, I mean that if one wins, the other must lose. This is the only kind of conflict that can fuel a story and keep it moving. As long as both of these characters are in active pursuit of their goals, the friction between them provides the energy your story needs to run.

When I'm talking about conflict in your story, this is the kind of conflict I'm talking about: narrative conflict.

Any other kind of conflict is **mundane conflict**, which commonly presents as humorous bickering or some kind of disagreement.

MUNDANE CONFLICT:
Conflict not based on goals

With mundane conflict, there are no goals involved. This kind of conflict is commonly based in philosophical or personality differences, or some kind of misunderstanding.

Have you ever seen the TV show *Moonlighting*? If your answer is yes, then you've experienced a whole truckload of mundane conflict. I'm not saying it's not delightful. There's a good reason why we see so much mundane conflict in our stories; it's *fun*. And having two people who disagree philosophically can *lead* to narrative (goal-based) conflict if they set themselves to mutually exclusive goals based on those disagreements, but it is not narrative conflict in and of itself. It's just regular, everyday, mundane conflict.

Which isn't necessarily a problem, as long as *all* of your conflict isn't mundane. There is absolutely a place in storytelling for banter and bickering between characters with personal or philosophical differences. What's important is that you can distinguish between these two kinds of conflict in your writing, because trying to fuel a story with mundane conflict is going to end in frustration for everyone involved, primarily you.

Before we move on, however, I want to spend a moment talking about a particularly pernicious form of mundane conflict called **false conflict**. This is a problem that appears as conflict, but is not, in fact, actual conflict.

There is a simple litmus test for false conflict: If an honest conversation between the two people involved would dissolve the conflict, it's false conflict.

FALSE CONFLICT:
Any conflict that would be immediately dissolved if the parties involved have an honest conversation

A classic version of false conflict is the "But She's My Sister!" trope. A man—we'll call him Mike—and a woman—we'll call her Beth— are starting up a romantic relationship. Everything's going wonderfully until Beth goes into town to buy Mike a gift and sees him leaving a restaurant with his arm draped over the shoulder of (*gasp!*) another woman.

Immediately threatened by this other woman and certain he's cheating, Beth goes to Mike's apartment, slashes all of his pillows, dumps the feathers on the floor, pours a bottle of vodka over them, and is about to light it all on fire when he walks in and says, "Beth, what are you doing?"

"You cheated on me!" Beth says.

Mike blinks twice in stupefied innocence. "No, I didn't."

Beth, not about to allow herself to be gaslit by this douchebag, says, "I saw you stepping out of a restaurant with your arm around a woman!"

At that exact moment, the woman steps into the apartment, holds out her hand and says, "Hi. I'm Andrea, Mike's sister."

If Beth had walked over to Mike and said hello as he and Andrea were leaving the restaurant, the resulting conversation would have prevented all of this. *That* is false conflict, and it is basically only useful in farce, and then only because we are laughing at the idiots who engage in it.

While we're here, let's take a moment to acknowledge that I just gave you an example where false conflict is actually central to the story aesthetic: farce. My goal here is not to tell you what you can and can't do. I just want to make sure that you, like the writers of *Frasier* who milked 11 seasons of hilarity from false conflict, make those choices with complete knowledge of what you're doing.

For writers who don't want false conflict, the conversation test is a pretty handy diagnostic to make sure you're on the right track.

All right; back to narrative conflict. Quick reminder:

NARRATIVE CONFLICT:
A goal-based conflict between a protagonist with a goal and an antagonist with a mutually exclusive goal

You have a protagonist and an antagonist who are locked in conflict. Let's use Indiana Jones and Toht from *Raiders of the Lost Ark* as an example. They both want the Lost Ark of the Covenant. Dr. Jones wants it in a museum, and Toht wants it to give Hitler greater power. This is a mutually exclusive conflict; both men want to possess it and control the Ark, but only one of them can.

One of my favorite things about narrative conflict is that, when you have it, your protagonist and antagonist don't have to hate each other. One doesn't have to be capital-G good and the other capital-B bad. They only need to have goals in opposition to each other.

Let's dive back into the Harrison Ford oeuvre for this next example. In *The Fugitive*, Dr. Richard Kimble escapes from prison because he wants to prove his innocence. Federal Marshal Samuel Gerard wants to bring Kimble back in because Kimble is a fugitive. It's nothing personal; Gerard just has a job to do. My favorite moment in this movie is when Kimble and Gerard face off in a water outlet pipe and Kimble says, "I didn't kill my wife!" and Gerard says, "I don't care!"

These two are not hateful to each other, they just have mutually exclusive goals. Kimble can't prove his innocence while in prison, and Gerard wants to put him back behind bars. Aside from that little detail, they might even be friends.

Earlier in this book, we went to the etymology of protagonist and antagonist—first in the contest or struggle, and pushing against in the contest or struggle—but those are about the meanings of the words. Here, we want to think of our protagonist and antagonist in terms of their role in the story; what it is that they *do*.

PROTAGONIST:
The character whose perspective directs the reader's experience of a story

ANTAGONIST:
The character whose goal blocks the protagonist's goal

You may recall that earlier in this book I talked about the three qualities that make a *strong* protagonist. The protagonist is the character whose perspective directs the reader's experience of a story; whose pursuit of an active goal escalates the central narrative conflict; and who has the most at stake should they lose that conflict.

Those are all true for building a *strong* protagonist, and we'll address that in more detail in the chapter on character. But the only absolutely non-negotiable quality that makes a protagonist a protagonist is that they are the character whose perspective directs the reader's experience of the story.

You might have also noticed that there's nothing in either of those definitions that requires either one of these people to be good or bad; that's a common dichotomy in our stories, but the classic protagonist as hero-antagonist as villain pairing is not required.

Which makes this a good time to talk about heroes and villains.

HERO:
The Good Guy

VILLAIN:
The Bad Guy

All right, that's an oversimplification, but that's pretty much it. The person who does the right thing for the right reasons; that's your hero. The person who does the wrong thing for wrong reasons; that's your villain.

While we typically associate protagonists with heroes and antagonists with villains, there is no narrative requirement that it shake out that way. Protagonists can be villains; there is nothing in villainy that is mutually exclusive with being our POV character whose dogged pursuit of a goal is fueling the conflict and structure. *Dr. Horrible's Sing-Along Blog* and *Megamind* are two examples of this approach to protagonism. In *Dr. Horrible's Sing-Along Blog*, we experience the story through Billy/Horrible's perspective, and he is a classic comic book villain;[6] same with Megamind. Often, stories like this end tragically (*Dr. Horrible*) to punish the villain, or feature a change of perspective in our protagonist (*Megamind*) to transform them into a hero, but not always.

In *Young Adult*, the protagonist, Mavis, is a disillusioned, middle-aged ghost writer who, throughout the course of the film, learns absolutely nothing. In the final scene where it seems like she's about to have a breakthrough, she instead retreats back into the familiar comfort of her own darkness. Mavis's internal central narrative conflict between the part of her that wants a better, more connected life and the part of her that wants to stay the same is resolved, so it's narratively legit. The story works. And in the end, Mavis's life *hasn't* changed, which in this case is what gives the story its meaning.

---

[6] Captain Hammer, Horrible's antagonist, is also a villain. He's just a villain pretending to be a hero. Fun, huh?

I know. I know. I said that how a world changes is what gives the story meaning, and now here I am, telling you the exact opposite?

Not exactly.

In the case of *Young Adult*, we have an unhappy character in conflict who finally resolves that conflict by choosing *not* to change. But there *is* a change, in that Mavis has consciously chosen to be this way; before, she just *was* this way. The change is the fact that she's made an active, conscious choice to be what she has always been.

Isn't that cool? I'm telling y'all, stories are *the shit*.

CENTRAL NARRATIVE CONFLICT

Now that we understand narrative conflict—goal vs. goal—let's talk about **central narrative conflict**, which is the narrative conflict upon which the structure of a story is built.

Let's rest here for a moment to absorb that.

CENTRAL NARRATIVE CONFLICT: A goal-based conflict upon which the structure of a story is built

Plain old narrative conflicts can exist on a lot of levels. Any conflict that's based on mutually exclusive goals is a narrative conflict. What creates a *central* narrative conflict is that it is the narrative (goal-based) conflict upon which the structure is built. Most stories will have a lot of conflicts woven into their fabric. Some of them will be mundane (no goals) and some will be narrative (goal-based), but *only one* will be the narrative conflict upon which the story structure is built.

This is the *central* narrative conflict.[7]

Let's run through all this conflict stuff again, just so we're clear.

Mundane conflict is any disagreement between characters in a story that is not based in mutually exclusive goals. It can be based on something as ephemeral as a bad mood or a too-spicy chicken wing.

Narrative conflict is conflict based in two mutually exclusive goals.

Central narrative conflict is a conflict based in two mutually exclusive goals upon which a story structure is built. It is because of this conflict that the world changes at the end of the story, which is the change that generates the meaning (narrative) of the story.

You can nest mundane and smaller narrative conflicts within a central narrative conflict; in fact, I recommend it. Conflict, like garlic, is not something you can have too much of.[8] Throw some philosophical differences (mundane conflict) into the middle of a scene-level narrative (goal-based) conflict with mild to moderate stakes which simmers inside the high-stakes goals that form the *central* narrative conflict of the whole story and... *chef's kiss.*

---

[7] There can be multiple complete stories in any one form; sub-plots or parallel stories in a movie or book; side-quests in a video game. For example, a book with multiple parallel storylines will have a different central narrative conflict which defines the structure of *each* parallel story. Think *Game of Thrones*, which has dozens of parallel stories going on per book, each of which has their own structure based on their own central narrative conflict. Story and narrative exist within form, but are not defined by it.

[8] Fight me.

Let's take the opening scene of *His Girl Friday* as an example of all three types of conflict in one space.

First, we have Hildy Johnson arriving at the offices of The Morning Post with a scene-level, moderate-stakes goal—to get Walter to leave her alone so she can move on with her life and marry kind, reliable, boring Bruce—and a story-level, high-stakes goal of getting Walter to pull her back into the newspaper game and stop her from marrying kind, reliable, boring Bruce and ruining the rest of her life. In the scene itself, Walter and Hildy argue about pretty much everything, but mostly about their marriage and how and why it failed. That's mundane conflict which, paired so nicely here with two other levels of conflict, works wonderfully.

Now, let's revisit the definition of central narrative conflict.

CENTRAL NARRATIVE CONFLICT: A goal-based conflict upon which the structure of a story is built

I'll have two chapters dedicated to structure in a bit, but it's important to remember that while conflict is conflict—a struggle in opposition—*central narrative conflict* is intricately woven into the main story structure, as it defines where the story starts, escalates, and ends.

What I mean is this:

The story starts when your central narrative conflict starts.

The story escalates along the line of your central narrative conflict; that's what builds your structure.

And the story ends when the winner of the central narrative conflict is decided.

How that ending changes the world is what gives your story meaning.

That's important, so put that in your back pocket; we'll return to it later. But before we can talk about the relationship between conflict and *structure*, we need to examine the relationship between conflict and *character*.

THE NARRATIVE CONFLICT FORMULA

I use a simple acronym to help my students remember how to identify or form a narrative conflict: PGAG.

PGAG
Protagonist/Goal vs. Antagonist/Goal

That means you've got a protagonist with a goal and an antagonist with a goal that is mutually exclusive to the protagonist's goal. By mutually exclusive, I mean that if the protagonist wins, the antagonist must lose. Conversely, if the antagonist wins, the protagonist must lose.

Now here's a twist that you might not be expecting; *it doesn't matter who wins.*

You may need a moment for this to sink in, but it's true; a story can feature a protagonist losing this central fight, this epic battle.

A story's structure (the sequence of events) tracks along the escalating central narrative conflict, and that story ends when the winner of that conflict is decided.

How it ends? Depends on the meaning you want to evoke. The conflict must be resolved—in other words, someone must win—for the story to end, but *who* wins is entirely up to you, which you will decide based on what you want that story to mean. Typically, readers like for the protagonist to win, because those stories create the meaning that good prevails, which people tend to find comforting, so most stories end with a protagonist who has earned that victory.

But that's just one way for a complete, legit narrative to play out. An antagonist can win and, as far as your story's narrative legitimacy is concerned, the narrative structure will be just as strong.

Let's revisit *His Girl Friday*. We have our protagonist, Hildy, who wants to move to Albany and marry her fiancé, Bruce. Our antagonist, Walter, wants Hildy to stay in New York, re-marry him and write for his newspaper. At the end of the movie, Hildy loses; she decides to stay with Walter and be a journalist. This works because all along, we know that what Hildy *says* she wants—to move upstate and marry Bruce—isn't what she *really* wants, even though it's her clear goal and she's clearly fighting for it.

We also have a secondary conflict in this movie, this one an internal conflict for Hildy, where she has to choose between the work she loves and the life she's trying to build with Bruce. In the end, she chooses the work and Walter. So, we have two narrative conflicts running side by side; the central narrative conflict is the external conflict with Walter, and the internal conflict is a secondary narrative (goal-based) conflict that supports the central narrative conflict.

The fact that we are rooting for Hildy to choose the work and Walter over dowdy old Bruce is what makes it palatable when the antagonist, Walter, wins in the end. We want Hildy to be a journalist, and we want her with Walter, so it doesn't sting so much that she loses out in the central narrative conflict.

Now, be warned. In some stories you try to analyze, the central narrative conflict may not be clear, and that's okay. Just because a book got published or a movie got made doesn't mean it has all its narrative ducks in a row. And remember; not every story has a strong narrative as its primary focus, and that is okay. Also, just because a movie or book or whatever is successful doesn't necessarily mean it has a narrative structure you can bounce a quarter off of.

Still, looking for these elements in the stories you engage with will help you to understand the concepts of narrative theory a little bit better. A weak or unclear goal for a protagonist can be the reason why a story doesn't work very well. And if the story you're looking at doesn't have these elements clearly established, then it's time to think about how you'd fix it. There's no better way to build your understanding of narrative than working your mojo on existing stories.

INTERNAL CONFLICT AND EXTERNAL CONFLICT

Remember how I mentioned earlier that Hildy from *His Girl Friday* has an internal conflict (Hildy vs. Hildy) riding alongside the external conflict (Hildy vs Walter)? Let's expand a bit on that and talk about the different *kinds* of narrative conflict that can fuel a structure.

It's possible you might have come across some basic types of conflict—person vs. person, person vs. themselves, person vs. society, person vs. nature—in your literary education at some point, but when it comes down to it, there are really only two categories of conflict: internal and external.

Either your protagonist is fighting themselves (internal conflict), or they are fighting someone/something else (external conflict).

Person vs. person, person vs. nature, and person vs. society are all **external conflicts**. What that means is that the source of the conflict is external to your protagonist; there's another force pushing back against your protagonist.

In *Guardians of the Galaxy*, Ronan wants the infinity stone to destroy the galaxy, and Peter Quill wants it to save the galaxy. Only one person can possess it at one time, and as long as Quill has the stone, Ronan will be on his tail, trying to get it from him. If we remove Ronan from the movie, then there is no conflict and hence, no story.

Internal conflict is your classic person vs. themselves. This means that the protagonist is causing their own problems; they want two things that are mutually exclusive, and they want both things equally. Often, internal conflicts break down to your protagonist's higher self vs. their lower self, and the two mutually exclusive desires are the expressions of that internal conflict.

In *Toy Story*, Woody causes his own problems because he wants to be a good toy to Andy, dedicating his entire existence to Andy's happiness, but he also wants to be Andy's favorite toy. In the beginning, these two desires are not in conflict, and all is well. But then Buzz Lightyear shows up and usurps Woody's position as Andy's favorite toy and now Woody's in conflict. If he puts Andy's happiness first, then he needs to let Andy play with Buzz. But if he puts his own happiness and sense of identity first, which requires that he is Andy's favorite toy, then he needs to get rid of Buzz by pushing him out the window.

You may be forgiven for thinking that Buzz is Woody's antagonist, but upon analysis, it's clear that Buzz is no antagonist. He's not doing anything to block Woody from a goal; Woody is blocking himself and creating all his own problems in the process. Buzz is completely oblivious to Woody, and that's how you know he's not the antagonist. He's not trying to pull Andy's attention away from Woody; he's just trying to fix his plastic spaceship.

Now there are other conflicts making the rounds in *Toy Story*, but the main story runs along this internal conflict, which makes it our central narrative conflict.

It isn't until Woody finally chooses to sacrifice himself so that Buzz can return to Andy, putting Buzz's life and Andy's happiness first, that the central narrative conflict is resolved. We spend the rest of the movie solving the problems that conflict created—first, being stuck at Sid's house, and second, getting back to Andy—but the central narrative conflict is over at that point.

Another great example of an internal conflict is *Roxanne*. It may seem as though the hot firefighter and rival for Roxanne's affections, Chris, is our protagonist C.D.'s antagonist, but he isn't. Chris isn't trying to block C.D. from telling Roxanne how he feels; it's C.D.'s own insecurities about his appearance that keep him hiding in the shadows and unable to express his love for Roxanne.

In both of these examples, it's possible for people to see external conflicts with Buzz and Chris as antagonists, but that doesn't work when you look at their motivations; neither of them are blocking our protagonists at all. When you have a situation like that, you can usually find the central narrative conflict internally.

Or you might not find a solid conflict at all, which again, just means that the writer(s) either failed to build a strong narrative conflict, or building a story with narrative wasn't what they were interested in doing, and that's okay.

Internal conflicts are always a person vs. themselves. While these conflicts tend to be a little less obvious than external conflicts, they are legitimate conflicts upon which a strong structure can be built.

External conflicts seem simpler and more direct, but they can get a little hairy when we get to person vs. nature and person vs. society. These are legitimate external conflicts, but they present complications that can make them tricky to navigate, because conflicts with a person as the protagonist and a person as the antagonist are just easier to wrangle. This is true for three reasons: *reaction*, *escalation*, and *personal investment*.

Reaction. The nice thing about an active, sentient, personified antagonist is that when your protagonist zigs, the antagonist can zag to block them. This is necessary because any conflict a protagonist can quickly sidestep isn't going to be a strong or lasting conflict; it's hard to keep that story in the air. If a protagonist is walking down the sidewalk, and there's some construction happening on the sidewalk that's blocking the way, the protagonist just switches to the other side of the street and goes on their way. But if a *person* doesn't want them to get where they're going, that person can go across the street and block them again. That's narrative antagonism.

Escalation. As the protagonist works to get around the antagonist, the conflict gets stronger; it escalates. The antagonist, whose goal may not have been about the protagonist personally in the beginning, becomes personally invested. They get angry, they work harder, they actively make things worse. In response, the protagonist works harder, gets angry, becomes personally invested if they weren't already. Without a person as an antagonist, it's harder to get the conflict to become personal, and to escalate.

Personal Investment. Those of you who are old enough to remember the ad campaign for the horror thriller *Jaws 4: The Revenge* may remember the tagline, "This time, it's personal." Now whether or not that idea helped the film's central narrative conflict to work better—I will never know because I'm on a 33-year streak of not seeing that movie that I ain't looking to break—it does speak to the idea that a personal investment is required to escalate a conflict… and in a longer series, you must Always Be Escalating. This means that if you start a conflict with an antagonist wanting to kill a protagonist, it's hard to escalate from there. What's worse than wanting someone dead? But, if you open with an antagonist simply wanting to take something the protagonist has, and upon being thwarted takes it personally and then wants to take the thing *and* make the taking hurt, you're going in the right direction.

Remember, however, that even though personified antagonists have the narrative benefits I've just laid out for you, that doesn't mean that person vs. nature or person vs. society *can't* work. What matters here is that whatever the protagonist is up against is unavoidable. Being unable to escape or avoid the source of the conflict is what matters, as the producers of *Jaws 4: The Revenge* knew well. The fact is that if the protagonist just stays out of the water, they can avoid conflict with the shark.[9] In order for a conflict to remain in the air, it must be kept in the air by both sides. This is easier (and more fun for the writer, I would argue) with a personified antagonist actively escalating the conflict, rather than passively existing around the protagonist. But the bottom line is this: If the conflict can remain in the air until the protagonist finally figures out a way to survive against whatever is trying to kill them (*nature*) or finds a way to meet their goal despite societal restrictions (*society*), you have a narratively workable conflict.

In Andy Weir's *The Martian*, scientist Mark Watney is stranded on Mars, a climate in which he cannot survive for very long, and he has to find a way to live long enough to be rescued or escape. The conflict functions narratively; Watney's exploits as he tries to "science the shit" out of the situation are engaging, and the character is funny and smart and entertaining to spend time with. Things get worse the longer he's there as time (a function of nature) is also working against him; his equipment will only hold out so long, and while he can extend his survivability on the planet, he can't last forever.

A person vs. society story is also possible, but because it's so easy to introduce a personal antagonist who represents society, or to turn it into an essentially internal struggle, usually these stories end up in the person vs. person or person vs. themselves conflict structure.

Probably one of the clearest examples of a person vs. society conflict is in Margaret Atwood's *The Handmaid's Tale*, in which we follow the

---

[9] Those of you out there yelling "Sharknado!" at me: I hear you. I see you. Shut up. ☺

suffering of a handmaid named Offred, who is forced to bear children for various Commanders, as she is one of the few fertile women left in a highly polluted and toxic environment. While there are various characters that block Offred during the story—the Commander's wife Serena Joy, and possibly Offred's lover, Nick—there is no single antagonist blocking her progress throughout. At the same time, this novel is more an examination of a society gone horribly wrong than a clear story with an ending that shows us whether Offred finally found happiness or not. We're left in an ambiguous space, where we discover what eventually happened to the society that held Offred down, but we don't really know what happened to Offred herself. This is one of those examples of a novel that is prioritizing other things over a clear central story, and that's okay. This doesn't detract from its value. It just doesn't have a strong central narrative conflict or story structure leading toward a resolution of that conflict. Valuable artistic expression exists with clearer story elements, and also with softer story elements.

But *How Story Works* is for writers looking to work with clearer story elements, and if you want to do that, you're going to need to understand goals.

GOALS

Narrative conflict is the fuel that keeps a story moving. But there's a core concept in narrative conflict that we've been casually throwing around without really looking at it too closely, and I think it's time we zoomed in for a closer look at that area: **Goals**.

We talk about conflict as a set of mutually exclusive goals—the protagonist wants something, the antagonist wants something, and the win state for one of them means a fail state for the other. It seems simple, but there are some things you need to keep in mind when building your goals, and like PGAG before, I use another handy acronym to keep us on track with goals: ASPA.

ASPA
Active
Specific
Personal
Achievable

Let's break this down, shall we?

ACTIVE

The first A in ASPA stands for Active. Remember when we were talking about Peter LeFleur in *Dodgeball,* and how he's a weak protagonist because he wasn't that interested in either saving Average Joe's or playing dodgeball to do it? The problem was that he wasn't active, he wasn't dedicated to making his goal happen. For most of the movie, he rode along on the energy provided by the group of supporting protagonists around him, who *were* actively in pursuit of that goal.

So, what makes a good active goal? For one, it's a *positive* goal. By positive, I do not mean that it's a selfless "save the world" kind of thing, although I guess there's nothing ruling that out, but in the narrative context I'm using "positive" to mean that your protagonist is in active pursuit of something, rather than passively wishing to avoid something.

For instance, many times in my classes when my students are pitching their final short film projects, I will ask them what their character wants, and they will often proceed to tell me what their character *doesn't* want.

"She doesn't want things to change."

"He doesn't want this girl to think he's a dork."

"They don't want to lose their job."

The second you hear yourself saying "they don't want *x*," you need to revisit your drawing board. While it's okay for the antagonist to start things, which means that your protagonist will be reacting to shots fired, once the conflict is in the air, the protagonist should be in *active* pursuit of a *positive* goal.

For instance, to save Average Joe's, Peter needs to win a dodgeball tournament with a $50,000 prize.

Active. Positive.

Now, there are ways to have passive, reactive goals that are about what the character wants—positive goals—but fail to consider the action the character should take to achieve that goal.

Look at Disney's classic *Snow White and the Seven Dwarfs*. We know Snow White is the protagonist because her name is on the marquee, but she's passive right down to her "I Want" song, where she wishes for the one she loves to find her. Later, we get another musical take on her passive desires, when she tells the dwarfs about her charming prince and how someday, her prince will come for her.

"Someday my prince will come?" Honey, no. If you want your prince, go find him.

Even when things start happening in the story, Snow White is reactive, rather than proactive. She passively accepts what happens to her, rather than making things happen. Let's run through her jelly-legged misadventures, shall we?

- She patiently waits for her prince to find her, rather than going out in the world to find him.

- Her evil stepmother sends the hunter to kill her, and Snow doesn't even take the initiative to run or beg for her life, she just screams and stands there, waiting for him to kill her.

- She doesn't run until the hunter tells her to run, and when she does, she stumbles across the dwarfs who give her a place to live. She wasn't looking for them, she hadn't heard of the dwarfs and gone in search of them hoping they'd give her refuge. She *stumbles across them*.

- Once she's in the house with the dwarfs, she's a little more active in that she, you know, cleans the house for them, but then evil Queenie shows up with a poisoned apple. Queenie tells Snow that it's a magical wishing apple, and this is the most active Snow gets. She takes a bite from the apple, hoping it will bring her prince to her, and instantly passes out.

- And then our protagonist is *functionally dead* for a chunk of the movie until the prince shows up and kisses her and wakes her up.[10]

Now, I know, back in 1937 American culture liked our women passive, but it makes for a bad movie, a bad protagonist, and a bad goal. Beyond kind of hoping that a man will come save her, Snow doesn't even have a goal in this movie; how is this woman the star?

Terrible story, guys. Just really, really bad.

---

[10] Don't kiss people who are sleeping or unconscious. It's sexual assault. I know you know that, but I still feel the need to say it, just don't do it. kthxbye

Okay, so we've covered the first A in ASPA: Active. Let's move on to the S, which stands for Specific.

SPECIFIC

Remember when we hit the avoidance/negative goal *she doesn't want things to change*? Aside from being passive as all get out, it's also vague. She wants *nothing* to change? Well, the date's gonna change. Her mood is going to change. The mileage on her car is going to change.

This is why a good goal is *specific*. Even better is a specific goal with a time lock.

Back to *Dodgeball*, we have Peter LeFleur, who has some issues with passivity as we discussed, but man, you can't beat the clarity and specificity of that goal—he has to find $50,000 in thirty days in order to save his gym. The goal is to save his gym, and that goal is both active and specific, and then on top of that, we've increased the specificity with a number he needs to hit, and a time frame within which he needs to hit it.

You can't always put a specific number on a goal and that's okay, but when you can it tightens things up considerably, because we can track a protagonist's progress, which automatically escalates the central narrative conflict as they get closer and closer to their goal. Remember the seven horcruxes in *Harry Potter and the Deathly Hallows*? Each one a little victory, and each one more challenging and dangerous than the last? Collecting a number of things to achieve the goal works nicely to keep things escalating.

Even better; it's specific.

But even without a number to hit and a ticking clock increasing the pressure and providing escalation, as we saw in *The Martian* as Mark Watney ran out of survival time on Mars, a specific goal is essential to a strong narrative conflict.

Let's see if we can massage the tragically ubiquitous *she doesn't want anything to change* goal.

First, let's just putter around with the semantics; at least *she wants things to stay the same* is positive. Not specific or active enough, but it's changing the context enough for us to move forward on our heroic search for narrative improvement.

But let's take that a little further. What, *specifically*, does she want to stay the same? Let's say, it's her boyfriend; she wants her boyfriend to stay with her.

Fine, but if the boyfriend isn't gone, then she's got her goal, and there's no *there* there. So, let's have the boyfriend skip town, maybe he goes to a medical conference in Paris, and then calls her to say it's over, he's met someone else. When our plucky heroine gets that call, she hops on a plane with the active, specific goal to get her Charlie back, and you've got *French Kiss*, one of the best romantic comedies ever made.

It's a very specific goal for a character who likes to play it safe, who wants things to stay the same. Make it active and specific, and you can work with that.

All right, next in the ASPA pipeline is the P: Personal.

PERSONAL

People spend a lot of their time trying to downplay their personal investment in things because caring means vulnerability, and people tend to be deathly afraid of vulnerability. But in our characters and our fiction, we *want* vulnerability—we will discuss that much more in the chapter on character. For now, it's important to remember that if your character isn't personally invested, your reader won't care, either. For this reason, your protagonist's goal needs to be of extreme personal significance. Remember when I said a strong protagonist has the most at stake? This is what I'm talking about.

It's *personal.* It *matters.* The protagonist may want to serve Thanksgiving dinner at a shelter for the housing insecure, a goal that is both active and specific, but it's not personal enough. She's a good person, volunteering her time, but she goes home to a warm bed and a fine life. Nothing is at stake for *her*, personally. But if she's there looking for the father who went missing when she was a child and who she believes has been coming to that shelter, then you're cooking with gas.

Sometimes we try to sideline the intense vulnerability of a personal goal by making it personal to someone who matters to the protagonist, and that's not a good move. Think about *French Kiss* and imagine that our protagonist Kate *wasn't* the one whose fiancé had skipped town to canoodle with some French floozie. Maybe it was her sister's fiancé. Well, that's great, but it's the sister whose life is falling apart, the sister who has the most at stake, the sister for whom this is absolutely and deeply personal. In this circumstance, Kate would be one level removed from the stakes, while her sister is at the center of catastrophe, which would make us feel pulled away from Kate and towards the sister as the protagonist. This situation is nowhere near personal *enough* for Kate.

Even when it's not literally life or death for our protagonist, it has to *feel* like life or death. In *French Kiss*, Kate is facing the death of everything she's built her life upon. This is so important to her that even though she's petrified of flying, she hops on a plane to get her Charlie back.

That's personal.

Okay, we've covered the ASP in ASPA, now we've got one final A to get to: Achievable.

ACHIEVABLE

A strong protagonist's goal must be achievable within the scale of the story you're telling.

For example, my screenwriting students are given a final project of fifteen pages, which will run about fifteen minutes of screen time when it's done. During the pitching process, I had one student come to me with an Irish family saga that starts three hundred years ago when the first Kenneally got off the boat.

Yeah.

No.

For a fifteen-minute short film, you've got about 48 hours max of story time for your conflict to start, escalate, and resolve. Ain't nobody got time for 300 years of family saga in fifteen minutes.

So, depending on the story you're telling—be it a feature film, a novel, a short story—you have to think about the scale of the story, and what kind of goal would be achievable within that scale. In a fifteen-minute short film, a protagonist can rescue a dog from an abusive owner. They can't charge the owner with abuse, put them on trial, and get them sent to jail—not without rushing your timeline so much that the audience loses the connection to the now of the story.

Another thing to consider when you're thinking about the achievable element of your protagonist's goal is whether the goal is really within the power of your protagonist to achieve. Is the goal world peace? Well, good luck on both scale and power considerations. Is the goal to force someone else to do something? Unless you want to give your character a gun or a blackmail scenario to significantly increase their power to control another person, then your character's power to achieve that goal is hobbled right out of the gate.

Let's return to Kate in *French Kiss,* whose active, specific, and personal goal is to make Charlie love her again. Well… that's not achievable. It's not in her power to make another person feel what she wants them to feel. Does that make it a bad goal?

In this case… no. Because she's *supposed* to lose. Because the whole point is that she has to realize that she can't make him love her, that she can't keep her life safe and protected and color-coded and alphabetized. Life is messy, and there are things outside her control, and she has to make her peace with that. That's the whole point of the story, and by giving Kate a goal she can't achieve, a fight she's not supposed to win, we actually play right into theme.

If it helps the story for your protagonist to fail in their goal, then mucking with achievability is okay, but it should be to the purpose of reinforcing the meaning of the story. Remember, it doesn't matter to the narrative integrity of the story if your protagonist wins or loses, just that the central narrative conflict is resolved one way or the other. If your protagonist is in pursuit of a goal they're supposed to lose, you can play around with achievability.

But if you want your protagonist to win, as most stories do, then you're going to want their goal to be achievable.

Now that we've got the basics of narrative conflict laid out, it's time to get to the reason why we need a strong central narrative conflict in the first place: to build our structure on.

5. STRUCTURE IN THEORY

Of all the parts of storytelling I've learned and taught over the years, **structure** is the most deceptive. It seems like a haven for crafties and a bog for magicals because there are all these principles to follow and definitions to learn and it seems so straightforward, like a blueprint.

That's the thing, though. It's deceptive. Yeah, there's a lot to learn, but once you learn it, you can bend and twist and manipulate structure to do pretty much anything you want. So magicals, don't crap out on me here. Just move through it, and you're gonna love it.

Crafties, you will also love it, because structure with all its principles and concept definitions gives you the very thing you want to put your back up against. All you have to do is follow it as prescribed, as though it's all rules, and you'll be good to go.

All right, now I've got some bad news for you: We're gonna start with Aristotle.

If all you know about Aristotle is that he's some dead Greek dude that started civilization or something, this idea might not be repellant to you. But if you are even a little familiar with his views on women or slavery, the fact that I'm starting with him might be bothersome. But here's the thing; Aristotle, for all his faults, and there were many, got us started thinking seriously about stories. And he's the reason why so many Western stories end up in a three-act structure even though three acts are not structurally superior to two. Or five. Or one.

It was because Aristotle went to a play and then thought and *wrote down*, "A whole is that which has a beginning, middle and end." He felt like that vague insight had enough intrinsic value that he wrote it down and told everyone he knew about it.

What I'm saying is… dude did not suffer from imposter syndrome.

But it's that idea—the beginning, middle and end—that led us in western storytelling to think in terms of three acts to every story. He also got us started talking about the ways in which stories allow us to process and feel our emotions (catharsis). He talked about the importance of a character's fatal flaw (hamartia), and the idea of peripeteia, the sudden reversal of fortune which you'll see pop up a few times in this book.

But mostly, he got us thinking about story structure.

In *Poetics,* he wrote, "Every Tragedy, therefore, must have six parts, which parts determine its quality—namely, Plot, Character, Diction, Thought, Spectacle, Song… But most important of all is the structure of the incidents."

He goes on to define what he's talking about with plot, character, diction, et cetera, and his definitions are vague as hell, but the part I'm interested in talking about is this:

Most important of all is the structure of the incidents.

Although I would argue with Aristotle on a lot of things, since stories are basically a meaning production system and structure delivers that meaning to us by showing us how the world has changed through the course of a story, I'd give him that one. But before I crack the cultural cement around narrative structure, let's back up a bit and dig a little deeper into what narrative structure actually is… and isn't.

WHAT PEOPLE THINK STRUCTURE IS

Something happens.

Then something else happens.

Then something else happens…

… and something else happens…

… and something else happens.

Then things stop happening, and the story is over.

Technically, this is true. Structure is absolutely a series of things happening. But, of course, as with pretty much everything else in the world, it's a little more nuanced than that.

WHAT STRUCTURE ACTUALLY IS

A protagonist wants something, so they take action.

An antagonist wants an opposing thing, so they block the protagonist.

The protagonist zigs; the antagonist zags.

The protagonist must try harder, do more, be better.

Lather, rinse, repeat, constantly escalating.

In the end, one side wins, and the conflict is resolved.

And the world is changed.

Structure escalates the central narrative conflict, making things worse and worse and worse, harder and harder and harder, until finally one side wins, at which point the central narrative conflict is resolved.

Afterward, we have the resolution, which shows us how the world has changed.

Remember how I said earlier that structure is a delivery mechanism for meaning? Well, structure is essential to that delivery mechanism. Meaning comes from change, and structure escalates the conflict that increases the pressure that creates the change, giving us meaning.

Our common idea of narrative structure—something happens, then something else happens, then something else happens, then things stop happening—doesn't take into account the specificity of what is happening. It doesn't acknowledge the importance that whatever happens must increase the conflict (pressure) in order to induce change, which delivers meaning.

With proper narrative structure, something happens, it sets off the central narrative conflict, the conflict escalates—the stakes get higher, the tasks get more difficult—and finally, the central narrative conflict is resolved, and the *world is different*.

Once again, let's revisit our definitions:

STORY:
A recounted event or series of events

NARRATIVE:
The meaning evoked by a story

STORYTELLING:
The art of building a story purposefully to serve a particular narrative

CONFLICT:
A struggle between two opposing forces

NARRATIVE CONFLICT:
A goal-based conflict between a protagonist with a goal and an antagonist with a mutually exclusive goal

CENTRAL NARRATIVE CONFLICT:
A narrative conflict upon which the structure of a story is built

All of these concepts have gotten us to where we are now. If you're struggling with any of what we've already done, go back and revisit that material until you feel like you've got a handle on it. Then come back and we'll move on to structure.

STRUCTURE:
The order in which the events of a story are sequenced

It's very basic; it's just the order of the events. But in the same way that there is conflict, and then there is narrative conflict, there is structure and then there is… **narrative structure**.

NARRATIVE STRUCTURE:
A structure sequenced purposefully to evoke a unified meaning or significance

Sequencing events in a particular way to evoke a particular significance; that's the juice behind narrative structure. The events must take our central narrative conflict from bad to worse, escalating with each beat until the climax, at which point a winner is decided and the central narrative conflict is finally resolved.

Sounds so simple when I put it like that, right? And yet, for me as a writer, structure is the thing I struggle with the most. The longer a project gets, the more expansive its scope, the more I feel like structure gets out of my control. I have more choices, more space to play, more side alleys to explore, and I sometimes get pulled off-track and confused about where I want to go.

Add to that the plethora of pre-built structures out there—Save the Cat, the Writer's Journey, the Hero's Journey, the Hollywood Formula, classic Aristotelian three-act structure, all of which tell us that there is One Right Way to build a story when clearly that is not the case—and the whole thing can make you want to curl up in the corner with a weighted blanket and some Nyquil and just take a damn nap.

Let's simplify by focusing on the most important thing you need to know about structure, and that is this: *Any* structure can work.

Let's say it again, because you're going to forget.

Any.

Structure.

Can.

Work.

The 40 beats of Save the Cat *can* work. The 12 stages of the Writer's/Hero's Journey? Sure, you bet. Wanna base a structure off the 22 cards in the Tarot's major arcana? Go for it. The 118 known elements of the periodic table? YES. And I would love that so if one of you sciencey writers wants to run with that, let me know when you're done because I want to read it.

At the end of this chapter, I'm even going to offer you a simple, incredibly common three-act, seven-anchor-scene (3/7) model you can use to both analyze existing story structures or to build a standard novel or feature-length film script but when I do that, please remember... this is not *the* structure.

It is *one* structure, one of millions out there you can build and use if you know the four essential steps in narrative structure, the four things your story structure needs to do. Remember SEE Change?

Yeah. That.

THE BASICS OF NARRATIVE STRUCTURE

1. **S**tart the conflict.

2. **E**scalate the conflict.

3. **E**nd the conflict.

4. **Change** the world.

SEE Change.

Now that last part, *change the world*, is the most important part of the whole thing, but it comes last, so we're gonna talk about it last. But tuck that away in your noggin. I don't want you to think it's not a big deal just because it's last. It's a *huge* deal.

But first, let's talk about what the other three elements of narrative structure must do to earn changing the world.

START THE CONFLICT

Conflict is essential to structure, and you cannot have a functional structure without it, so we need to establish our conflict, and then get it in the air.

By "starting the conflict" I mean that both narrative parties (protagonist and antagonist) are actively engaged in the conflict. They both know their goals, and they are both in pursuit of their goals.

For instance, when Little Red Riding Hood goes into the forest and meets the Big Bad Wolf, we have conflict. Red is on a mission to go see Granny and was given strict instructions from her mother to stay on the path. Wolf wants to distract her so he can get to Granny first. He steps in her way, blocking her from following the path.

Conflict launched.

ESCALATE THE CONFLICT

Remember when I talked about how it's easier to have a personified (*person v. person* or *person v. themselves*) conflict as opposed to a non-personified (*person v. nature, person v. society*) conflict? This is why.

Personified conflicts *escalate*. The protagonist zigs, the antagonist zags, and something is now at risk that was not at risk before.

That's escalating.

Red says she has to stay on the path, and Wolf says, "Okay. I'll walk with you, then." Red is uncomfortable with this, but she allows it because… well. It's Wolf. What's she gonna do? Along the way, they pass by a small clearing full of wildflowers and Wolf tells Red to go pick some for Granny, who deserves some beauty in her drab, old cabin. Red is drawn by the flowers, and wants to pick them, but was told not to stray from the path.

"Your mother will never know," drawls Wolf, his voice the very soul of menace feigning innocence. "Who's going to tell her?"

Red has a bit of an internal struggle, and then figures it won't hurt to step off the path just for a moment. The flowers *are* pretty, and though Granny's eyesight is poor, she does love the smell. Red wanders off to pick the flowers, and Wolf chuckles and rushes down the path to Granny's. When Red has her bundle of flowers tucked away in her basket, she turns back to go to the road, and sees that she's alone. For a second, she's relieved that he's gone, but then she realizes what Wolf's up to, and she runs down the path to save Granny.

Conflict escalated. It's not just that the Wolf has been blocking Red from her goal, but now he's going after Granny, and there is more at stake.

END THE CONFLICT

Once the conflict is escalated—made worse, with more at stake—it must be resolved. A winner must be decided.

Red shows up at Granny's house to discover Granny in bed, with the covers pulled up tight. Red notices, however, that Granny looks a bit different.

"What big eyes you have," Red says.

"The better to see you with," says Granny.

"What big hands you have," says Red.

"The better to hug you with," says Granny. "Now come a little closer so I can give you a big hug."

Red moves closer, tentatively. "What big teeth you have," Red whispers, afraid.

"The better to eat you with!" says the Wolf, who grabs her and pulls her into the bed, opening his jaws for a bite.

Red screams, and a woodsman hears her. He rushes to the cabin and rescues Red, then chops Wolf open, letting Granny—miraculously unhurt after being swallowed whole—out of the wolf's belly.

And that horrifying scenario is what qualified as a happy ending a few klicks back. Trust me, you don't want to hear the earlier versions of this tale; this is absolutely Disneyfied compared to *that*.

Happiness lives on a sliding scale, y'all.

CHANGE THE WORLD

I want to do a bit of review here, and reinforce a couple of ideas, because we're at a very important place in our narrative studies.

So once again, from the top:

A story is a recounted event, or series of events, and narrative is the meaning evoked by a story.

Let's interrogate that for a moment; how do we know what the meaning is?

We know *because of how the world has changed,* and structure—how the events of a story are sequenced to evoke a particular meaning— shows us the world at the beginning of our story and contrasts it with the world at the end of our story. **Structure shows us how the world has changed, and change determines what the story means**.

When I say "the world has changed" that can be as simple as a protagonist who has grown within a story. The "world" of a story is as much about the interiority of the protagonist as it is about the literal world in which that protagonist lives. For everyone else in the protagonist's world, things might be exactly the same as they were the day before, but if your protagonist has changed internally then their world has changed, and *how* their world has changed gives the story meaning.

How has the world changed at the end of Little Red Riding Hood? We don't really know, because the traditional children's story just kind of ends once the wolf is killed. But even without written scenes showing us how Red's world has changed, we can guess.

For one, innocence has been lost, which is a massive theme in storytelling, because once we realize that the world is not what we thought it was, we are forever changed by that knowledge. Red will never, ever trust a wolf again, or anyone she meets on the road. She will always be on her guard. She will always look twice at Grandma before trusting that she is, indeed, Grandma.

Red's *traumatized,* y'all. And what does that tell us? What does that change mean? It means innocence is temporary. It means that eventually, we will all meet with a metaphorical wolf on a metaphorical path to a metaphorical safe place and realize that we are not, in fact, ever safe.

Ever.

Yeah, Nietzsche's whole "don't look into the abyss or the abyss will look back into you" feels super relevant right about now, doesn't it?

Now's a good time to back away from the edge of existential dread for a moment and get back to our narrative theory.

Little Red Riding Hood is a functional narrative because it does four things.

Starts the central narrative conflict.

Escalates the central narrative conflict.

Ends the central narrative conflict.

Shows how the world has **changed**.

That's what structure does.

NARRATIVE UNITS

We've reviewed everything we've already learned to get us here; now, we've got some new terms to define so we know what we're talking about with structure. If structure is merely the sequence of events—and it is—then how do we express *events* in fiction?

EVENT:
A moment of change

Think of an empty white room. Just four white walls, a floor, and a ceiling. You can stare at that white room for a long, long time, and if there is no change, then it is fundamentally the same as it ever was; there has been no event.

But if the ceiling opens up and drops a red ball into the center of the room, we have an event. Something has changed.

Events are moments of change. Story is a recounted series of events. Structure is how those events are sequenced.

And **narrative units** are how we express events within a story.

NARRATIVE UNIT:
An expression of events within a story

We're going to define and track these narrative units from small to big. Narrative units work a little like Matryoshka nesting dolls, only instead of just one doll inside each bigger doll, you might have a bunch. We are defining our narrative units to work actively toward the progression of a story's central narrative conflict, to structure the story from the catalyst of that conflict to its resolution.

First, we'll summarize the narrative units, and then we'll go into more detail on what they are and how they work.

A **beat** is a single unit of narrative change.

A **scene** is a sequence of chronologically continuous beats, culminating in a larger narrative change.

An **anchor scene** is a scene which significantly and purposefully escalates the central narrative conflict.

An **act** is a sequence of scenes which work together to alter the relationship of the protagonist to the central narrative conflict, bringing on a new approach toward or perspective on that conflict.

All narrative units are expressions of narrative change; any of them can stand on their own as an individual **composition**.

COMPOSITION:
A narrative unit that launches, escalates, and resolves a central narrative conflict and then shows how the world has changed

Writing flash fiction? Then the **scene** is your composition, if it has launched, escalated, and resolved a central narrative conflict, and shown how the world has changed.

A one-act play? Then the **act** is your composition.

A novel, a TV episode, a feature-length movie? These are composed of multiple acts, which are composed of multiple scenes, which are composed of multiple beats, and they are compositions if they complete the story.

And finally, we have a **series**, which is a sequence of compositions which work together to tell connected stories within a single world or thematic landscape.

BEATS & SCENES

Now that we've got our units defined, let's go a little deeper and see some examples of how they work, beginning with **beats**. A beat is a single unit of narrative change. Beats are the moments within a scene that indicate progression; something happens within them, which allows the next thing to happen. They are steps in a staircase, rungs in a ladder.

To help illustrate how beats work and what they are, I'm going to use a scene I wrote as an example for my screenwriting class.

EXT. PLAYGROUND - DAYTIME

A LOVELY FALL DAY. CHILDREN are running,
screaming, laughing. PARENTS are
supervising. Life is idyllic, and mundane.

A DAD, mid-40s, stands to the side,
ignoring his SON on the swing set while he
pokes at his phone.

>   SON
>   Dad! Watch me! See how high
>   I can go!

ROSIE, 6, sits nearby in the sandbox,
making bucket-shaped blocks of sand with
her orange PLASTIC BUCKET, and watching.

>   DAD
>   Yeah, that's great, buddy.

From behind, we see SLENDERMAN (age
indeterminable) step beside the dad.
Slenderman is UNNATURALLY TALL AND THIN. He
wears a PRISTINE BLACK SUIT and has the
complexion of the dead.

Throughout, we never see all of
Slenderman's face in full focus; we do see
the uneasy reactions of the people around
him.

Slenderman watches the kids on the swings.

The dad glances at Slenderman, gives a
casual, fake smile and glances away. Then
he slowly raises his eyes back to
Slenderman, his expression horrified,

although he doesn't seem quite sure why.
Still, he can't seem to look away...

The dad puts the phone in his pocket, still
staring at Slenderman.

He swallows.

> DAD
> So... you... uh... you got
> a kid out here?

Slenderman's voice is casual, but strange.
Almost as if it's been slightly auto-tuned.

> SLENDERMAN
> No.

> DAD
> (eyes on Slenderman)
> Time to go, buddy!

The dad manages to pull his eyes away from
Slenderman, and he hustles toward his son.
He pulls the kid off the swing gracelessly,
in a panicked hurry.

Slenderman stands and watches.

> SON
> But I don't want to go yet!
> You said we could stay a
> whole hour! Why are we
> leaving now?

The dad glances in Slenderman's direction
and seems a little confused himself.

<pre>
                    DAD
     I... uh... I gotta work,
     buddy.
</pre>

The dad hustles the kid away.

Here we have the first beat; we see Slenderman at the park, and through the reaction of the other dad, we see that Slenderman is creeping people out. Our first unit of narrative establishes our scene status quo; Slenderman wants to be around people, but he makes them uncomfortable.

Referring to our white room example from earlier in this chapter, this is our white room, our status quo.

<pre>
Rosie glances up at Slenderman, who
continues to watch all the other families.
She dusts off her hands and picks up her
orange plastic bucket, then walks over to
Slenderman and stands next to him.

                    ROSIE
          You don't got a family?

Slenderman turns toward her a bit.

                    SLENDERMAN
          No. I don't.

Rosie stands there a moment, in silence,
thinking.

                    ROSIE
          I don't got a dad.
</pre>

                    SLENDERMAN
          I'm sorry to hear that.

                    ROSIE
          Yeah. He ran off like a
          goddamned dickless wonder.
            (beat)
          That's what my mom says.

                    SLENDERMAN
          It's his loss.

                    ROSIE
          Yeah. That's what my mom
          says, too.

Rosie points toward the neighborhood homes
visible nearby.

                    ROSIE (CONT'D)
          I live in that house over
          there. The one with half
          the roof is green. You see
          it?

Slenderman takes a moment, shielding his
eyes from the sun to look.

                    SLENDERMAN
          That looks like a nice
          house.

                    ROSIE
          It's a piece of goddamned
          crap.

                    SLENDERMAN
          Is that what your mom says?

```
                    ROSIE
        No.
```

This is the second beat of narrative change; an event has happened. The young girl has seen him and talked to him and not been afraid; Slenderman is able to connect with her.

This is our red ball dropping from the ceiling; a change in the status quo. Now, we have a new status quo: Rosie is special, and might be someone who can really see Slenderman.

```
                    SLENDERMAN
        Okay.
          (beat)
        It must be nice to have a
        house and a family.


                    ROSIE
        I guess. I have a brother.
        I don't like him. He bosses
        all the time. You don't
        have a house, even?


                    SLENDERMAN
        No.


                    ROSIE
        No brothers or sisters? No
        mom?


                    SLENDERMAN
        No.


                    ROSIE
        Xbox?
```

Slenderman chuckles, charmed.

                    SLENDERMAN
No.

                    ROSIE
Well, hell, mister, what do
you got?

                    SLENDERMAN
I have... a job.

                    ROSIE
Oh. What's your job?

                    SLENDERMAN
I watch.

                    ROSIE
Sounds boring.

                    SLENDERMAN
Well, I'm supposed to be
better at it. I'm supposed
to talk to people, to
connect. To understand
them. But people seem to be
afraid of me.

He brushes off his jacket sleeve.

                    SLENDERMAN (CONT'D)
Does this suit seem off-
putting to you?

                    ROSIE
Yep.

Slenderman nods.

Here's another beat; Slenderman confides in Rosie that he's supposed to connect with people, but can't. We also see that Rosie does see that he's weird; she's just not bothered by it. Rosie has also shared vulnerability with Slenderman, sharing about her father (in the previous beat) and her brother.

Shared vulnerability between people is what allows them to connect. True in life, true in fiction.

So now, the red ball in our white room begins to shake, showing that there's some kind of force coming from the hole in the ceiling from which it dropped.

                    ROSIE
          Knock knock.

                    SLENDERMAN
          I'm sorry?

                    ROSIE
          You say, "Who's there?" I
          say, "Knock Knock," and you
          say, "Who's there?" and I
          say, "Apple," and you say,
          "Apple who?" Don't you even
          know how a joke works?

                    SLENDERMAN
          I think I can follow your
          instructions.

                    ROSIE
          Okay. Knock knock.

                    SLENDERMAN
          Who's there?

ROSIE
Apple.

SLENDERMAN
Apple who?

ROSIE
Knock knock.

SLENDERMAN
Who's there?

ROSIE
Apple.

SLENDERMAN
Apple who?

ROSIE
Knock knock.

SLENDERMAN
(hesitating)
I don't see where this is
going.

ROSIE
Banana.

SLENDERMAN
Banana... what?

ROSIE
(harsh whisper)
Banana who... say, "Banana
who?"

                    SLENDERMAN
          Oh. Yes. Certainly. Banana
          who?

                    YOUNG MAN'S VOICE
          Rosie!

Both Rosie and Slenderman look up to see
FRANK, a lanky fifteen-year-old kid who's
all bones and length and way older than his
years, rushing toward them.

                    FRANK
          I swear to God, I turn my
          back for one minute--

                    ROSIE
          Mom said I can come out
          here to play when I want
          to. Long as I can see the
          house from where I'm at, I
          can play. And there's the
          house.

He grabs her hand and looks up at
Slenderman, clearly battling his own
discomfort.

                    FRANK
          You stay the hell away from
          my sister, you hear me?

Slenderman and Rosie are bonding, becoming friends, sharing jokes.
But they get interrupted; the only person Slenderman has been able
to connect with is being taken away.

The red ball floats in the air, back up toward the ceiling.

>   ROSIE
>   Shut up, Frank. He's my
>   friend. His name is...
>   What's your name, mister?

Slenderman looks at her, his head cocked.
Name? Huh. He doesn't seem to have thought
about that.

>   ROSIE (CONT'D)
>   His name is Jimmy.

Slenderman gives a slight nod of
acceptance; he is now JIMMY.

Slenderman now has an identity. *Jimmy.* This is a huge change; being
named changes him fundamentally.

The red ball changes in color; it is now yellow.

>   ROSIE (CONT'D)
>   And he's coming for dinner.
>   He doesn't have no family.

>   FRANK
>   *Any* family.

>   ROSIE
>   You know how Mom likes to
>   invite people with no
>   family.

                    FRANK
          That's at Thanksgiving.
            (to Rosie, but looking at Jimmy)
          Say goodbye, Rosie.

He pulls Rosie away, and she turns back,
tossing her orange bucket at Jimmy, who
catches it easily.

                    ROSIE
          You can bring it back when
          you come to dinner!

Frank pulls on Rosie even more, moving
faster, and Rosie fights him to look back
at Jimmy.

                    ROSIE (CONT'D)
          We eat at six o'clock,
          every night. It's taco
          night! I'll tell Mom you're
          coming!

Frank yanks her, not hurting her, but
making his point clear.

Rosie angles herself stubbornly to wave at
Jimmy.

From behind, we see Jimmy's hand rise. Five
unnaturally pale fingers extend and then
curl, one by one, back into his palm.

In the other hand, he clutches the handle
of the orange plastic bucket.

Jimmy now has an identity. He has a plan to spend an evening with a family. He has a friend. He has an orange bucket. **His world is wholly different from what it was when the scene started.**

The now-yellow ball flies toward the hole in the ceiling and disappears. The white room is once again empty, but the hole in the ceiling is still there, and the absence of the now yellow ball is felt. The room may look the same as it did when we started, but it is fundamentally changed, and can never go back to what it once was.

And that is how a series of beats, using small incremental changes, becomes a scene, a unit of larger narrative change.

SCENE:
A series of chronologically continuous beats pulled together to create change within a story

That series of beats I shared with you combine to form a complete **scene**; one unit of change composed of smaller units of change.

Now that we've got beats and scenes down; let's move to acts and compositions.

ACTS & COMPOSITIONS

Scenes are a series of chronologically continuous beats that work together to create larger change, and acts can be defined in a similar way. Acts are a series of scenes (not necessarily chronological) that work together to create a more significant change. In addition, **an act denotes a fundamental change in the relationship of the protagonist to the central narrative conflict.** What makes a change fundamental is that it cannot be reversed; once this change happens, it cannot *un*-happen. If this feels a little muddy, if you're unsure of how acts break out in a story, return to your central narrative conflict; when the protagonist's relationship to that conflict changes so much that they cannot go back, you've got a completed act.

ACT:
A series of scenes that work together to fundamentally alter the protagonist's relationship to the central narrative conflict

When we get to anchor scenes, you'll see how a single strategically-placed scene can mark a fundamental change that transitions the story from one act to the next. Some of those anchor scenes will mark a **turning point** that stems from everything that came before it, culminating in a specific choice the protagonist makes in response to the central narrative conflict that changes everything.

In a one-act story, that change can be the thing that decides the winner and resolves the central narrative conflict. In a multi-act story, it means that we've created a significant change in the protagonist's relationship to the conflict *without* resolving that conflict.

Remember, a narrative unit is only a *final* narrative unit—or **composition**—if the central narrative conflict has been resolved. Otherwise, we just keep moving into the next narrative unit.

Which brings us to compositions.

Whether it's a single scene that launches, escalates, and resolves a conflict, or a novel, film, or TV episode, if a central narrative conflict has been resolved, that's a composition.

COMPOSITION:
A narrative unit that launches, escalates, and resolves a central narrative conflict and then shows how the world has changed

And then, when we have multiple compositions linked by theme or existing within the same story world, we've got a **series**.

SERIES:
Multiple compositions linked within the same story world or thematic landscape

A series can launch, escalate, and resolve its own greater central narrative conflict as well, and I think the best series do exactly that. But often, they don't; they're just a string of compositions that exist within the same story world or thematic landscape (think anthology television series like *The Twilight Zone* or *Black Mirror*). What makes something a series is that we have multiple final narrative units— multiple compositions—within that story space.

Now that we've established and defined our narrative units, let's take a look at our sample structure.

6. STRUCTURE IN PRACTICE

Every writer starts out as a mimic. That means we see something done a certain way, and then we do it that way. When I teach my novel revision class, I tell my students that whether or not they know anything about three-act structure, it is likely already present in their stories to some degree. The class participants never believe me, and then I teach them three-act structure with seven anchor scenes and their eyes grow wide as they see that framework within their own stories. They didn't intend to write three acts with seven anchor scenes; they just absorbed them through engaging with so many stories structured that way, and that structure embedded itself into their stories without them even knowing it.

The three-act structure is in no way superior to a one-act structure for a shorter story, or a five-act structure for a longer one. In the same way you buy the sheets that fit your bed best, you work with the structure that fits your story best. That said, whenever I teach this structure, people lock onto it like it's a life vest in deep seas, so let me say, once again, that this is *one* structure that will work; it is not *the only* structure that will work. It is not even the *best* structure; it is simply *a* structure.

If your structure accomplishes SEE Change (start the conflict, escalate the conflict, end the conflict, change the world) then it works. Three-act structure is just one way to do that.

BASIC THREE–ACT STRUCTURE

To get started with structure, which escalates the central narrative conflict, we need to create a central narrative conflict for our protagonist that we can then escalate through the story's structure. For that we have a formula, as you may recall from our discussion of conflict.

PGAG
Protagonist/Goal vs. Antagonist/Goal

From jump, you need to know the protagonist and their goal, and the antagonist and *their* goal. These goals, as we talked about in the chapter on conflict, must be mutually exclusive; if one wins, the other must of necessity lose. That is your conflict lock.

The three acts and the seven anchor scenes (let's call this a 3/7 structure to simplify) will blossom from that fertile ground; they will track the central narrative conflict, escalating it throughout the story, and then landing it with a climax (the final battle in which a winner is decided) and finishing with a resolution (a scene or series of scenes that shows us how the world has changed, for better or worse).

With that in mind, let's start with a big picture overview of the three acts.

ACT I

The first act introduces our characters, sets up the world, launches the central narrative conflict, and escalates it to the point where the protagonist makes an active choice to engage with the conflict and

94

the antagonist. That active choice to engage changes the protagonist's relationship to the central narrative conflict because they go from oblivious or ambivalent about the conflict to fully engaged and ready to fight.

ACT II

Act II continues to escalate the central narrative conflict, making things worse, challenging the protagonist in ways the protagonist is not prepared for. The first response of the protagonist will be to do things the way they've always done things, but this time, their comfort zone will not serve them well; this will push them to change tactics, to try something new. The second act is about putting pressure on the protagonist, showing them that they must learn, improve, and dig deep in order to succeed. The second act is where the stakes are raised, and loss becomes unacceptable. The second act ends when the protagonist again makes an active choice to try harder, be bolder, step outside of their comfort zone, and take a risk. This choice will be defining; once they make this choice, going back is no longer an option. They are absolutely locked in, and ready to fight to either the literal or metaphorical death.

ACT III

In the third act, everything moves faster, the conflict comes to a head, and the final battle is underway. A winner is decided during the **climax**, which again changes the relationship the protagonist has to the central narrative conflict because now it's over, and they have either won or they have lost, but they are different for having engaged in the fight. This moves us into the resolution, where we see how our protagonist and/or the world has changed because of this fight.

ACTIVE CHOICES

You may have noticed some of the language I use when talking about the first and second acts; each of them ends (ideally) with an **active choice from the protagonist** to push the conflict ahead. Every time the protagonist makes that active choice, their relationship with the conflict changes; it escalates. That's where the ideal act turns are; when the protagonist's relationship with the conflict *escalates*.

All right; let's get a little more detailed now.

ACT I

In your first act, you must:

- Introduce your protagonist and make your reader care about them;[11]

- Introduce your central narrative conflict, and by the end of the first act, have your protagonist committed to it;

- Set up the world, tone, supporting characters, antagonist; and

- Get your central narrative conflict launched, preferably in the first scene.

All this while being entertaining and making it look easy.

It is NOT easy.

---

[11] You'll learn how to do that in the chapter on character.

The first act sets the stage, establishes a protagonist and, by the time you're transitioning to the second act, has outfitted them with a goal that is **active**, **specific**, **personal,** and **achievable**. Then, the protagonist feels the opposing pressure from an antagonist with a mutually exclusive goal. At the end of the first act, the protagonist has decided, for once and for all, to engage with that conflict, and to fight back.

ACT II

The second act raises the stakes and escalates the central narrative conflict.

Escalation can sometimes be a confusing concept, so let's take a moment and play here for a bit.

Maybe this is where the antagonist starts to take this conflict personally, and it's no longer enough to win the goal; they want to *hurt* our protagonist while they win.

Maybe our protagonist desperately wants a promotion and knows they're in competition with some other people for this job, so they sabotage the competition... then they discover that the person they've been secretly in love with all this time is in competition for the job, and they've been sabotaging the person that means the most to them.

Or maybe an amateur detective is trying to solve a murder, but in the second act, she discovers that the murderer might be her husband.

These are all escalations, where the problem becomes more complicated, and the stakes get higher. There's suddenly more to lose if things go wrong. Escalations set up choices for our protagonist, and nothing heightens the flavor of a narrative more than an active choice. Does our amateur detective continue on her path to find the murderer, even if it means that her husband goes to jail? When we force our protagonists to make the tough choices, we learn who they really are, and that adds texture and nuance to your story.

The second act ends when our protagonist is faced with an active choice; do they continue to fight, even though the stakes are so high as to at least *feel* like life and death stakes, even if they aren't *literal* life and death? If the protagonist pushes forward at this point in the narrative, they cannot go back again; they are locked in. They've hit the point of no return, and that launches us into the third act.

ACT III

In the third act, the protagonist has pushed forward despite all the complications, consequences, and escalations. The final battle happens and a winner is decided. And now, because of the events of this battle, the world has changed. Our protagonist has paid a price for pushing onward. They lose the promotion but win the love of their life; or she solves the case, but sends her husband to jail, and loses the life she had before. A win can be bittersweet; there's a price to be paid, but the price is worth it.

Or... maybe it's not worth it. There is no rule against a bummer ending. Maybe our amateur detective chooses to protect the husband, and not solve the murder. She keeps her life as she knew it, but she can't go back to the way it was, and we know she's going to suffer for making that choice.

Those are the basics of how acts work. Now we're going to break acts down further into the seven **anchor scenes**, the big moments that track the escalating central narrative conflict across the three acts.

THE 7 ANCHOR SCENES

In the last section, we talked about how the three acts work, giving us an overview of the general movement of the story. We start with the central narrative conflict launching and escalating in Act I. We make it worse and raise the stakes in Act II, challenging our protagonist to go outside of their comfort zone in order to win the day. And we climax and resolve it in Act III, resolving the central narrative conflict and showing how the world has changed.

Now we're going to zoom in a bit and look at our seven anchor scenes, but before we do, let's spend some time with our definitions, starting with a reminder about scenes:

SCENE
A series of chronologically continuous beats pulled together to create change within a story

Now, let's talk about what makes an anchor scene special.

ANCHOR SCENE
A scene that significantly escalates the central narrative conflict.

Let's take a moment and talk a bit about the difference between a scene and an anchor scene. A scene is a collection of chronological beats that create a significant change within a story… but they don't necessarily escalate the central narrative conflict. They might nudge it forward a bit, or they might be part of a sub-plot or parallel narrative, but they are not significant enough to qualify as an anchor scene.[12] An anchor scene is a major structural point in the story; something big happens, pushing the central narrative conflict into a new space. A pre-built structure will give each of those anchor scenes a specific job to do in the narrative, and once they've done that job, things have changed in the story world.

Three of the seven anchor scenes are also **turning points**:

TURNING POINT:
An anchor scene where the protagonist makes an active choice to escalate the central narrative conflict

The first turning point anchor scene transitions the story from Act I to Act II, and the second turning point anchor scene transitions the story from Act II to Act III. The last turning point anchor scene comes just before the climax, launching the story into the final beats of Act III. Having the protagonist make active choices to escalate the central narrative conflict at these turning points makes for a stronger story and a stronger, more active protagonist.

Below is a diagram of how the seven anchor scenes work in an idealized three-act structure:

---

[12] A sub-plot is a secondary, shorter storyline with its own escalating central narrative conflict. A parallel narrative is a completely separate, but just as prevalent, storyline with its own escalating central narrative conflict.

3/7 STORY STRUCTURE

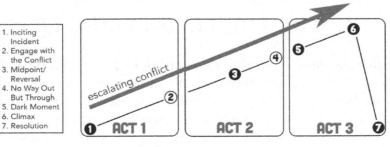

1. Inciting Incident
2. Engage with the Conflict
3. Midpoint/ Reversal
4. No Way Out But Through
5. Dark Moment
6. Climax
7. Resolution

escalating conflict

ACT 1   ACT 2   ACT 3

② ④ = turning point/active choice

Did you notice my use of the word "idealized"? That's because this is a roadmap, not a strict set of rules. You can alter the plan at any time if it serves your story. You can change the specific job that an anchor scene does. Or you can follow this faithfully. Just remember that this structure, like any pre-built structure, exists to serve the story. When it stops serving the story, you can improvise and that is perfectly fine.

Most three-act stories will have moments that track along these general guidelines, but there will be variation in how they land, and in their function. As you're tracking acts and anchor scenes in the fiction you engage with, don't be freaked out if the story you're working with doesn't map exactly. You'll see variations of this structure in different story forms, but in movies specifically, you're likely to see this 3/7 structure pretty often.

And the reason for that? It works.

All right. Let's get to it—the seven anchor scenes. To minimize confusion in the following anchor scene descriptions, I'll be using she/her pronouns for the protagonist and he/him pronouns for the antagonist, but I would like to say here that characters, like people, exist fully everywhere on the gender spectrum and are not limited to a binary representation.

1: THE INCITING INCIDENT

The first anchor scene is called the **inciting incident**. This is the first moment that the protagonist feels the influence of the antagonist pushing back against her goal. Now note, the antagonist doesn't have to be physically present. Your protagonist doesn't even need to know who the antagonist is; at this point, only the *influence* of the antagonist has to be felt.

The inciting incident should happen **as close to the start of the story as possible**. There are many things, as the writer, that you've got to do at the start of the story. You've got to establish the world and the characters and the rules and the stakes; it's a full plate. With all of that going on, do not feel like you also have to launch the conflict on page 1. That said, you don't want to wait too long, or you risk losing your reader. Do your best to balance all the demands of your opening scenes, and launch that conflict as soon as possible.

After the inciting incident, Act I continues with the conflict slowly escalating and the protagonist learning more about her situation. Other characters and storylines may be introduced, and then we get to the end of Act I, which is capped with the second anchor scene: Engaging with the Conflict.

2: ENGAGING WITH THE CONFLICT

At the end of Act I, we have the second anchor scene, **engaging with the conflict**. Up until now, the protagonist may have known that someone or something was getting in between her and her goal, but she was still figuring things out. By the end of Act I, she knows that she's being actively blocked and she commits to her goal,

actively choosing to engage in the central narrative conflict to pursue her objective. This is also the **first turning point of the story**.

Once our protagonist has chosen to engage with the conflict, we move into Act II. Things are moving along, our story's gaining some momentum, the central narrative conflict continues to escalate, and the stakes are getting higher. There's more potential consequence, more at risk, and the antagonist is being thwarted and working harder to obtain his goal and block the protagonist.

3: MIDPOINT/REVERSAL

In the middle of Act II, which is also about the middle of the story, we hit on the third anchor scene, aptly named **the midpoint**, sometimes also known as **the midpoint/reversal**.

The midpoint is where new information is obtained that changes how the protagonist sees the conflict. This could be that our protagonist learns something new that recontextualizes the conflict for her, making her even more committed to her goal. Or it could be that she's knocked back hard by the antagonist and realizes now how dangerous or powerful he is. This information may be so shocking that it alters her understanding of her goal and her motivation for pursuing that goal may broaden, or the goal itself might even evolve.

What's important is that even as the goal evolves, it remains mutually exclusive from the antagonist's goal. As long as that's the case, you're good to go.

4: NO WAY OUT BUT THROUGH

Next, we move on to our fourth anchor scene, a turning point anchor scene that transitions us from Act II to Act III, sometimes called the **point of no return**. I think of it as **no way out but through**.

Here, our protagonist again makes an **active choice** to continue on with the battle, even though the stakes are so high, even though she's been challenged so much that she's not sure she can win. Despite how hard it all is, she actively chooses to move forward, because the consequences of going back are not acceptable to her. This is the point where her motivation to achieve her goal becomes stronger than all the reasons to run and hide, and she chooses to fight.

Now, we're in Act III, when we crest the hill of our story terrain and start sliding downhill with increasing speed.

5: THE DARK MOMENT

Almost immediately after moving into Act III we get to the fifth anchor scene, **the dark moment** when all seems lost, death is imminent, but our protagonist continues fighting. She doesn't quit. This fifth anchor scene is the story's final turning point, pushing the protagonist toward the climax and resolution.

6: THE CLIMAX

We move immediately from the dark moment into the sixth anchor scene, **the climax**, when the final winner in the central narrative conflict is decided. Our protagonist sees the fight through to the end. Maybe she wins, maybe she loses; either scenario is narratively legit. What's important in the climax is that the victor is decided, once and for all.

7: RESOLUTION

Finally, we move into the seventh anchor scene, **the resolution**. The resolution being designated as one anchor scene is a bit misleading, because the resolution is usually not one big scene, but a series of small scenes showing us how the world has changed now that the battle is decided. However, even as a group of scenes, this part of the story functions to achieve one objective; to process what happened and understand the new world left in the wake of those events.

In the resolution, we look to what has changed in this story to understand its meaning.

ILLUSTRATING THE 7 ANCHOR SCENES

To illustrate the seven anchor scenes, I'm going to expand on our simplified version of Little Red Riding Hood from earlier in this book. We've already done Red's story with the basic SEE Change structure, and I'll map that four-point structure—Start the conflict, Escalate the conflict, End the conflict, Change the world—to the 3/7 structure to illustrate the concepts behind the anchor scenes, but also so you can see how you expand a story from a simple structure to a more complex one.

ACT I: INCITING INCIDENT (START THE CONFLICT)

Red comes inside after doing her chores to find Mother crying at the kitchen table. Red asks what's going on; Mother says that Grandma is ill. Mother wants to go take care of Grandma, but there's so much to do at the farm; she can't take that kind of a trip. Red says she can go, but Mother hesitates. It's too dangerous. Red promises to be careful. Mother agrees with a sigh of combined relief and apprehension. As she loads up a basket with food and medicine, she gives strict instructions; don't talk to anyone, don't stray from the path, and get to Grandma's before dark. Red promises to follow her mother's instructions, takes the basket and heads out. The walk is pleasant. It's a sunny day, no one is around and Red is enjoying herself.

After a while, she notices some movement and glances around. Nothing. She walks a little more and hears a whistle.

She looks around.

Nothing.

A few more steps and suddenly a beautiful dark gray wolf appears just off the forest path, walking in pace with her.

"'Morning," Wolf says.

Red says nothing.

"Nice day, don't you think?" Wolf asks.

Red says nothing.

"Luckily, I'm not the kind of guy who takes things personally," Wolf says, and slows down, letting Red continue on her way. Red is relieved, but then she hears singing...

It's Wolf.

Red stops to listen. His voice is deep and gravelly, but the melody has a surprising bounce to it. Her feet are eager to dance, but Red holds still.

When he finishes the song, she asks, "Who taught you to sing?"

In an instant, Red realizes that she broke one of her mother's rules; she spoke to him. But his song was so lovely, and she wants to hear it again so she can remember it, she thinks Grandma would love the song… but Mother said not to talk to *anyone*. Red starts away again, eyes on her feet to be certain she doesn't stray from the path. If she keeps her head down and stays away from the edge of the path, maybe the wolf will just go away…

"What's the rush?" says Wolf, walking just off the path, keeping pace with Red. "Don't you like my song?"

Red shakes her head.

"I know you can speak," says Wolf. "You spoke to me just a minute ago."

Red keeps walking, eyes on the path.

"My mother taught it to me," Wolf says, and wanders off, ambling lazily into the woods without looking back.

Red glances up to see him retreat and continues on her way. She keeps her feet solidly within the bounds of the forest path and gets to Grandma's before dark.

That night as Grandma sleeps, Red sits by the fire, trying to remember the wolf's song. She hums a bit to herself, then hears a hint of a gravelly voice from deep in the darkness, singing that tune. She goes to the window and strains to listen, but hears nothing more than the wind.

- o We've launched Red's internal conflict; she wants to obey her mother, but she also wants more of Wolf.

ACT I TO ACT II TURN: ENGAGING WITH THE CONFLICT (ESCALATE THE CONFLICT)

The next day, Red is picking flowers in Grandma's garden. The sky is blue, the sun is shining, and she sings the song to herself quietly.

"What terrible song is that?" a voice says. Red jumps and looks up; it's Wolf.

"It's *your* song," Red says.

"That is not my song," Wolf says. "You got all the notes wrong."

"Well, I like my version just fine, and anyway—" Red catches herself, once again, talking to Wolf and stops. Wolf grins.

"Your mother said not to talk to anyone on the *way* to Grandma's," Wolf says. "But now, you're here. The rules have changed."

Red looks at him. "How do you know what my mother said?"

"That's what all the mothers say."

Red buries her face in her flowers so Wolf can't see her smile.

"There are prettier flowers just over there," he says, nodding toward the vibrant field of wildflowers blooming off the forest path.

Red meets Wolf's eye and says, "Now, what would my mother have to say about *that?*"

Wolf shrugs. "Nothing, if she never finds out."

Red gets up, brushes the dirt from her knees, and hugs her basket of flowers to her chest. "Maybe tomorrow," she says, and allows a sly smile.

"Well, then, maybe tomorrow I'll teach you how to sing that song right," Wolf says.

Red heads back into the house, feeling a small thrill in her certainty that he is watching her walk away.

> o   Red is engaging with the conflict; she's not rushing to disobey her mother, but she's having fun flirting with Wolf.

ACT II: MIDPOINT/REVERSAL (ESCALATE THE CONFLICT)

The next day, Red goes outside and starts down the forest path, walking by the field of wildflowers. She pauses at the edge of the forest path. She hums the song, as best as she can remember it.

Wolf doesn't show up.

Red lifts her foot, then hesitates and puts it back solidly on the path. She hums a little louder and looks off toward the trees that line the edge of the field. Behind them is darkness, but she doesn't sense any movement there.

He's not there.

He's not coming.

Disappointed, Red goes back inside the house.

That night, Grandma starts to run a fever. Red puts cold cloths on her forehead and gives her the medicine Mother sent, but nothing works. It's late, but Red doesn't feel like she can wait until morning. She puts on her red cloak and grabs a torch, then heads out to find the doctor.

She's barely out of sight of the house when Wolf shows up.

"Hey, Red," he drawls. "Awfully late for a good girl like you to be out and about, isn't it?"

"Leave me alone," Red says and moves faster down the path. Wolf's tone goes from playful to serious.

"What's wrong?"

"I need to go get the doctor," she says, her voice brittle. "Grandma's sick. I think she's dying. Nothing I do helps. She's…" Red glances back over her shoulder at the house, the unthinkable crossing her mind. She looks back at Wolf. "She's alone."

"Go back," Wolf says. "I'll get the doctor."

"But—"

"Go!" he says, and disappears into the night. Red hesitates, then rushes back to Grandma's house. Grandma is still alive, but suffering, and Red goes from Grandma's side to the window, worried about how phenomenally stupid she was to ever trust a wolf. But soon, she sees a dim light on the path, moving closer. It's a lantern.

It's the doctor.

The doctor gives Grandma some medicine and the fever comes down. In the morning, Red makes them all breakfast, and Grandma seems to be doing better. The doctor leaves. Grandma naps.

Later in the day, Grandma is still napping, and Red is bored. She putters around the house for a little while, but then goes outside and walks purposefully off the path and into the field of wildflowers and starts to pick them. Once she has an armful, she glances up at the forest's edge and sees movement in the dark shadows.

Wolf steps out of the forest but doesn't move closer. He just looks at her.

She looks back. Her heart races. She feels a trickle of sweat at the back of her neck.

He turns and goes back into the forest.

She turns and goes back into the house.

- o The midpoint/reversal: Wolf honored her trust, and did as he said he would. Red wants him.

ACT II TO ACT III TURN: NO WAY OUT BUT THROUGH (ESCALATE THE CONFLICT)

Grandma is almost all better. She tells Red to go back home so that Mother doesn't worry. Red doesn't want to go right away. She likes it here, in the woods. It's so much more… peaceful than in town.

Grandma gives Red a knowing look. "You have to go back," Grandma says. "But someday when I'm gone, this house will be yours and you can stay here all the time."

Red is horrified at the thought and jumps up to hug Grandma. "I don't want your house without you in it!"

Grandma hugs her back and says, "Don't fight nature, child. You'll lose."

"I don't know about that," Red says, teasing. "I'm pretty stubborn."

Red packs up her things, and Grandma fills her basket with food and wine for Mother. Red heads out on the forest path. When she's almost out of sight of the house, she turns to wave, but sees that Grandma has already gone inside.

Red pauses on the path. She looks out over the field of wildflowers, to the forest's edge.

She glances back at the house.

And then… she runs. She runs off the path, through the field, to the edge of the forest where the line of trees stand like soldiers on guard duty. She stops and stares into the darkness. There are shapes there in the darkness, but she can't make them out. She reaches out her hand into the shadows and a voice says, "Are you sure you want to do that?"

She gasps and pulls her hand back. Wolf watches her from a few yards away.

"It's rude to sneak up on people," she says.

"It's rude to go where you don't belong," he says.

"It's as much my forest as yours," she says.

He laughs. "That's not even close to being true." He moves toward her. "But if you'd like… I can show you."

Red feels a thrill rush through her, followed by a stark fear. She glances behind her, and realizes she can't even see the forest path from where she is.

She's spoken to the wolf. She's gone off the forest path. And now, here she is, at the edge of darkness. But there's no going back now, is there? She's not going to just go back on the path and go home now like a good little girl… is she?

"Show me," she says.

He steps in front of her and walks slowly backwards, moving into the shadows.

Her eyes locked on his, she follows.

> o No way out but through. Once Red has broken two of the three rules, she has to break the third. She has to know.

ACT III: DARK MOMENT (ESCALATE THE CONFLICT)

Wolf doesn't speak as Red follows him deeper and deeper into the forest. It's mid-day, she knows it's mid-day, but forest shadows make it feel like dusk. The bright red of her cloak is now dark, like blood. And the wolf, who appeared charcoal gray in the daylight, now has a silver shimmer to his coat, making him look like he's made of starlight. He leads her through an area of thick branches and she has to crawl on her knees to enter his lair. The ground is covered in soft pine needles, and the space smells sweet and earthy.

"Sit," he says, and she does. It's so dark, she can barely see him. The air is thick and close, completely silent. He begins to sing the song, but it's different. Before, it was playful and fun. Now, it is plaintive and melancholy. She feels suddenly tired, and lies down on the ground. He curls up next to her, and his body is so warm that she instantly falls into a deep, dreamless sleep.

When she wakes up, she's alone. Where there was very little light before, there is none now.

"Wolf?" she whispers, her voice cracking. There is no sound, and fear rushes through her. She knows she is alone, in the forest, in the dark.

He left her.

Her eyes have adjusted a bit to the darkness, just enough that she can grab her basket and find her way out of the lair, but once she's out, she's not sure which way to go to get back to the field of wildflowers. She rushes through the forest. A tree branch grabs at her cloak, pulling it off her but she doesn't stop. She runs, breathing hard, spikes of panic shooting through her chest. She can feel eyes on her, lots of them, but nothing chases her as she runs.

Whatever is in that forest is letting her pass.

She makes it to the field, and it's way past dark. Red doesn't know which way to go. Home, to Mother? Or back to Grandma's? Should she call for Wolf? Where did he go?

She rushes through the field, the wildflowers and weeds slapping at her shins. When she gets to the forest path, she's about to head toward home when she hears a noise coming from Grandma's house.

Oh god. Oh god. Oh god. Her mind can't form any other thoughts as she runs.

   o   Dark moment. Red already knows what has happened, but she's going to Grandma's anyway, because she has to know for sure.

ACT III: CLIMAX (END THE CONFLICT)

Red bursts through the front door, but everything is silent. The fire is still going in the fireplace. Dishes are neatly put away. Nothing out of place. Red starts to relax, and even laughs at herself for allowing her imagination to run off with her.

Everything's okay.

Everything's fine.

She sets her basket on the floor and calls out.

"Grandma?" she says. "I'm sorry. I did something so stupid and I think I'm going to just stay the night here and go back in the morning, if that's okay."

The door to the bedroom opens, and Red turns with a smile.

And there is Wolf, in the doorway, just watching her.

"What did you do?" she whispers, her heart rate picking up again.

Wolf says nothing.

"What did you do?" she screams, and runs past him into Grandma's room.

It's empty.

"Where is she?" Red asks.

"She's gone," Wolf says.

"Where?" Red asks, her voice quivering.

"Don't ask a question you already know the answer to," Wolf responds.

Red sits on the edge of the bed, clasping the bedspread so tight in her fists that her fingers start to hurt. "How could you?"

"Stop pretending, Red," Wolf says. "You knew I was a wolf when you let me in."

Red stares at the floor, her throat choked as tears blur her vision. "I didn't let you in."

"Oh, come on," Wolf says, smirking at her one last time before turning his back and ambling away. "Sure you did."

Red sits on the edge of the bed, staring down at the floor. Slowly, she pulls her grandmother's quilt around her and falls back into the bed, where she silently cries until, finally, she falls asleep.

- o Red's conflict was always internal; she wanted to obey her mother, but she also wanted to see what was beyond the forest's edge. When she did that, she grew up, but there was a cost. Now, as she pulls her grandmother's blankets around her, she accepts that the girl who obeyed is gone. That battle is, finally, over.

ACT III: RESOLUTION (CHANGE THE WORLD)

A few weeks later, Red sweeps the living room of Grandma's house, which is now hers. She shoos the dirt out the front door and raises her hand up to shield her eyes from the sun as she looks out to the field of wildflowers. She can barely see the forest's edge from the stoop.

She goes back inside, leaving the door open. A light breeze flows through the house as she ambles to the kitchen. As she washes the dishes, she sings the Wolf's tune.

Plate.

Plate.

Mug.

Spoon.

She sets them all in the rack to dry, then turns toward her open front door and wipes her hands on her apron. Wolf stands at the threshold, watching her as she pulls the apron strings free at the small of her back.

"'Morning," she says, and heads to the bedroom, not looking back to see if Wolf will follow her.

Because she knows he will.

> o The world has changed. Red has gone from girl to woman. She has lost innocence, but she has gained her own power. She knows exactly what Wolf is, and she chooses to be with him, but on her own terms now. She may never trust him again, but he will never trick her again, and she lives peacefully within that watchful truce.

REVIEW: ANY STRUCTURE CAN WORK

Because so many stories, especially movies, are told in 3/7 structure, it is very easy to look at that and forget that any structure can work as long as it can SEE Change:

1. **S**tart the conflict.

2. **E**scalate the conflict.

3. **E**nd the conflict.

4. **Change** the world.

ADVANCED STRUCTURE

Before we move on to the chapter on character, I want to take a moment to say that one of the beautiful things about the SEE Change structure is how modular and extensible it is. I'm going to briefly touch on how it can contract or expand to fill the space it's been given, but since this is an introductory guide to story, I don't want to get too far into the weeds here. For now, learn the basics, but later, here are some things you'll be able to do following these simple principles of structure.

Short fiction. The intensity of your conflict depends upon how much story it needs to hold up. In short stories and flash fiction, you have the opportunity to zoom into what might seem like a small conflict… say, a person in a store trying to decide between comfortable or stylish shoes. That simple internal conflict can keep a one-scene story afloat, and a smaller conflict can work really well as a metaphor for something larger.

Parallel structures. You can have two stories with two separate protagonist-antagonist pairings and two central narrative conflicts entwined around each other. Parallel structures lend themselves well to flashback stories where you've got two stories in two separate timelines intercut and reflecting thematically upon each other. Romances, where you've got a storyline for one half of the romantic pair, and a separate storyline for the other, will often use parallel structures. Or, you can have two separate stories happening in separate spaces in the same timeline and crashing together at different points to intersect and provide big moments for each storyline; but note, they don't have to be the same anchor scene. A climax for one parallel storyline might be the midpoint/reversal for another. *Game of Thrones* is an example of this kind of storytelling, with multiple, staggered, parallel stories all happening alongside each other.

Non-linear structures. Non-linear structures will follow a thematic, rather than a chronological, escalation. You can pop around in time, revealing your theme in bits and pieces until the entire puzzle is visible to your reader, who will then put it together. In this case, your climax can happen early in the story, but your reader won't understand it as the climax until the end; so structurally, the climax occurs when the reader knows it has occurred. Mind-bending. *Memento* is a good example of this kind of thing.

Nested, or episodic, structures. This is most common to television and comic book series, in which there's a bigger storyline being worked out over multiple episodes. Each episode will be a complete narrative unto itself, with an escalating central narrative conflict that is resolved by the end, but the episodes themselves also push forward the season- or volume-level central narrative conflict, which resolves in the final episode of the season or issue of the volume. *Buffy the Vampire Slayer* and *Breaking Bad* are good examples of a nested structure.

Now that we've laid out how conflict and structure work, let's move on to the most important thing you will ever learn to write: character.

7. CHARACTER

Can you believe we haven't defined character yet? That's because character is one of those concepts that seems so obvious as to not need definition.

Those are the things that need definition the most.

CHARACTER
A fictional representation of a human

Seems simple but… what is a human? Red and Granny and Mother from our take on Little Red Riding Hood are all humans, right? So, they are characters. Easy peasy.

But… what about Wolf? Also a character, but not textually—meaning, through a literal reading of the text—human so… does he count as a character?

"Of course!" you say. "Duh."

Okay. So Wolf is not human, but he is a character, which is a fictional representation of a human so… shit. We know Wolf is a character… how do we know?

We know because of coding.

CODING

Stories are, at their core, always about human experience. When we talk about character as a fictional expression of a human, that includes anything *coded* as a human.

CODING
When a thing is textually one thing, but meaningfully or representationally another

Metaphor is an example of fictional coding. We are using one thing—say, a zombie—to represent another thing—say, the ways in which people are easily manipulated *en masse* to dampen their critical faculties so they behave in ways they might not as individuals.

Why do we code? If we want to talk about a thing, why can't we just talk about that thing? Well, because things are complicated. When we code, we can isolate one thing that we want to talk about without taking on all the other complications that might come with that thing.[13]

If we want to talk about the ways in which group think overtakes individual thought in a particular society, we need to talk about all the values that society holds and how those values work, like in Atwood's *The Handmaid's Tale*. If we want to talk about the pure destructive effect of that group think, we attribute it to a virus that overtakes people and makes them monsters, so that we can talk about the effect

---

[13] The word "thing" is hellishly vague and you know how I love specificity, but when I say "thing" I mean… anything. *Every*thing. People. Concepts. Objects. You can code with anything.

without spending too much time talking about why and how the effect happened.

That is the value of coding and metaphor; it allows us to look deeply at one idea and experience it without the complications inherent in that idea that might otherwise distract us.

The things that make characters human—their desires, their weaknesses, their vulnerabilities, their strengths—are the things that so grab our interest because they *are* us, in one way or another. When it comes to characters that are aliens, monsters, mythological gods or talking wolves, we are doing the same, but with human representation. Even if the characters are not *textually* human, if they are sentient, they are always *coded* as human.

Why do we do this? Because stories are always about human experience, and human experience is a vast area. By comparing a human to a zombie, or a wolf, we give ourselves the ability to zoom in on one area of human experience and talk about it with specificity and focus. Our daily lives as humans are complicated as all get out. Utilizing coding and metaphor in our fictional characters allows us to focus. We make it possible to hop into the character and live their experience, which brings us back to the ultimate magic of storytelling: narrative transport.

NARRATIVE TRANSPORT

George R. R. Martin wrote in *A Dance with Dragons*: "A reader lives a thousand lives before he dies … The man who never reads lives only one."

I'm with him, with the understanding that anyone of any gender who engages with any form—be it a novel, movie, TV show, video game, graphic novel, audiobook, comic book, whatever—is considered a reader.

But back to Martin's point; we engage in stories for a number of reasons, but primary among them is to *live* an experience. Remember when we talked about narrative transport?

NARRATIVE TRANSPORT:
When a reader's current reality fades away, and the reader lives for a time within the reality of the story

Narrative transport transforms a story into an actual lived experience. Have you ever read a story about falling in love, and then felt the same feelings you felt when you actually fell in love? That's what I'm talking about. There are a lot of emerging studies on this, the most notable from neuroeconomist Dr. Paul Zak, which show that cortisol, oxytocin and dopamine are elicited by stories, but you don't need a scientist to tell you this is real. You've felt it. You've cried when a fictional character has lost something beloved. You've been consumed by tension and stress when a hero on screen is hanging from a catwalk by one finger. You've sighed when fictional lovers kiss. Our brains, our bodies... they don't know the difference between what we're reading about and what we're experiencing, which makes a fictional experience *also* a lived experience.

Characters are the gateway to that lived experience because we hop into their bodies for a while and live through it all with them, *as* them. Isn't that amazing?

Look, just because it happens every day and we're used to it doesn't make that *not* magic.

This is why character is the most important pillar of narrative craft. If we are to hop inside the body of a character, we have to *believe* in that character, we have to experience that character as real (enough) that the narrative transport will work. Therefore, building our characters is the most important thing we do as writers.

CHARACTER CATEGORIES

Characters fall into three main categories: protagonist, antagonist, and supporting.

PROTAGONIST:
The character whose perspective directs the reader's experience of a story

ANTAGONIST:
The character whose goal blocks the protagonist's goal

SUPPORTING CHARACTER:
Every character in a story that is not the protagonist nor the antagonist

That's the simplified version; let's go a little deeper into how these different types of character work to keep a story moving.

PROTAGONIST

As we discussed in the chapters on conflict and structure, a story's central narrative conflict is based on a protagonist and an antagonist in pursuit of mutually exclusive goals. How that central narrative conflict escalates throughout the story provides the structure, which breaks into acts and anchor scenes that continuously escalate that conflict.

Identifying the protagonist in any given story is usually pretty easy. They are the main character, or the character whose perspective directs the reader's experience of a story. That is the essential quality. But a strong protagonist has two other preferred qualities as well; they provide the motive force for the story through their pursuit of a goal, and they have the most at stake if they fail to achieve that goal.

Let's take these on one by one.

The protagonist is the character whose perspective directs the reader's experience of the story.

In order for a protagonist to be a protagonist, the character must meet this requirement, which is why it is deemed essential. To be the "character whose perspective directs the reader's experience" means that the reader is seeing the story world through this character's eyes, experiencing the story world as that character experiences it.

While it may seem like we're taking in objective reality while engaging with a story, that's not really the case. We are always seeing the world through the lens of our protagonist, the same way we experience the real world through our own lenses. Those lenses can feel like they're not there influencing how we read the story, so part of being a critical reader means you don't forget that reality is being shaped by the lens through which you are looking, and that is not a complete and objective viewpoint. It is simply the viewpoint through which you are experiencing this particular conflict.

This is why it's so fun to see a familiar story through a different perspective, such as Gregory Maguire's *Wicked*, which looks at the events of *The Wonderful Wizard of Oz* through the Wicked Witch's perspective, who is the protagonist of Maguire's version. This is also why so many television shows have a *Rashomon*-style episode, inspired by Akira Kurosawa's film of that name, where we see the same events dramatically altered simply by changing the perspective character.

The protagonist provides the motive force for the story through their pursuit of a goal.

Remember PGAG? Protagonist + Goal vs. Antagonist + Goal? Well, the protagonist should be actively in pursuit of their goal, thus providing the motive force for the story. Remember Hildy from *His Girl Friday*? It is her active pursuit of her goal—to get Walter to sign the divorce papers so she can marry Bruce—that launches the story and keeps it going.

Often, protagonist problems stem from a protagonist who is passive and reactive, rather than actively moving the story along. By giving your protagonist a strong goal, you keep them in action, and they drive the structure, just the way the Story Gods intended.

However, this is a preferred quality of a protagonist; it's not essential. You absolutely can tell a story without the protagonist in pursuit of anything, but it will be a harder story for you as a writer to tell, and probably not as engaging for the reader to read. No goal means no central narrative conflict; no central narrative conflict means a structure that doesn't have a direction to follow. Without that structure, it's harder to keep a story's momentum going. The longer the story, the harder it will be.

The protagonist has the most at stake if they fail to achieve their goal.

The last consideration in building a strong protagonist is having a good sense of what's at stake. A strong protagonist will be the character in the story with the most at stake personally; they have the most to lose if they fail to achieve their goal.

This is another preferred, but not essential, quality. When your protagonist has the most to lose if everything fails, we as readers are most engaged with that character's situation. Remember when we talked about Kate in *French Kiss*? How if she went to France to get her sister's fiancé back, it wouldn't be as engaging? This is why; when the protagonist has the most at stake, the goal becomes immediately personal, which is one of the qualities that builds a good goal.

Let's revisit our protagonist elements in *Dodgeball*. Peter LeFleur— our main protagonist—owns Average Joe's gym, which he's going to lose if his team doesn't win the dodgeball tournament and thus the money to get Peter out of default on his loan.

Peter is the character through whose perspective the reader experiences the story; absolutely. He also has the most at stake if he loses the fight; it is, after all, his gym and his livelihood.

But he doesn't care much. He's not that invested. This is why the story needs his group of misfits, who need that gym because it's the only place where they belong, in order to make Peter care. He cares about them, so he pursues the goal.

This is what I mean by essential protagonist qualities vs. preferred protagonist qualities. A protagonist is defined by perspective; a strong protagonist also has the preferred qualities that allow you to build out the rest of your story in a way that is narratively strong.

Now let's talk about our other main character in storytelling; the antagonist.

ANTAGONIST

I love antagonists. They are so fun to write, mostly because they only need to do one thing: block the protagonist.

That's it. For an antagonist to function narratively, they just have to be locked in a mutually exclusive conflict with the protagonist—they have to be actively blocking the protagonist's progress, creating conflict, putting the protagonist under pressure, and forcing the protagonist to dig deep in order to win the day.

This is at the heart of why writing antagonists is so much fun; there really are no other rules. Protagonists are a bear to write; they have so many things to accomplish narratively, *plus* they have to be sympathetic and compelling. (We'll get to that in a minute.)

An antagonist, however, can be *any* kind of character you want. They can be funny. They can be truly evil. They can be sympathetically evil. They can be capital-G Good. They can even be acting out of love and care for the protagonist or someone else. The only thing they *must* do is have a goal that is in conflict with the protagonist's goal. There's so much freedom in writing an antagonist. If you accomplish that one thing—make them block the protagonist—you can do anything else you want, and there are so many options. Here are just a few examples of the kinds of antagonists you can write.

THE BENEVOLENT ANTAGONIST

This is an antagonist who loves and wants the best for the protagonist, it's just that what the antagonist thinks is best may not be what the protagonist needs or wants. This antagonist is often a parent, romantic partner, or friend who thinks they know better, and will fight the protagonist, saying it's for the protagonist's own good. Mother Gothel in Disney's 2010 Rapunzel story, *Tangled*, is a good example of a benevolent antagonist… at least, in the beginning. She becomes another kind of antagonist through the course of the story, and that's *another* awesome thing you can do with antagonists: You can switch their type midstream.

Oh my god, y'all. They are so much fun.

THE DOPPELGÄNGER ANTAGONIST

The Doppelgänger antagonist is an antagonist who is similar to the protagonist in a lot of ways, but because of one fatal flaw or one wrong choice, they go down the wrong path and end up crossing the protagonist. Belloq from *Raiders of the Lost Ark* is an example of this; he's a secondary antagonist in the movie, but he's also an archaeologist like Indiana Jones, interested in furthering knowledge through the excavation of priceless artifacts. His greed, however, gets the best of him and he goes down a dark path, a path that Indiana is in danger of going down himself.

THE SYMPATHETIC ANTAGONIST

This is someone who's just doing their job—a police officer, a health inspector, a social worker—but the nature of that job puts them at odds with our protagonist. Remember when we talked about the scene in the drain pipe between Richard Kimble and Samuel Gerard in *The Fugitive*? I didn't kill my wife/I don't care? We love Samuel Gerard in that movie. He's charming, smart, funny… and just doing his job.

Those are just a few flavors of antagonist; there are many, many more out there, and when you have an afternoon to burn, I recommend a Google search to find more.

And that brings us to…

SUPPORTING CHARACTERS

Don't let the simplicity of this huge bucket of characters make you think they're no big deal. The community of people that surround your antagonist and protagonist are the basis of the world, and they can be just as rich and deep as any main character. They are the protagonist's community—friends, family, colleagues, townsfolk. They are the antagonist's minions.   or sub-plot protagonists or antagonists for parts of the story. Don't make the mistake of thinking you can just dash off a supporting character with little effort or thought; the best stories have supporting characters who are built as carefully and thoughtfully as any protagonist or antagonist.

We've defined our three basic kinds of character: protagonist, antagonist, and supporting. Every character you write will fall into one of these three base categories. These categories, however, speak only to their function in the grand scheme of the narrative structure.

What you need to understand now is how to build a *strong* character. For that, a handy tool is the character triangle.

THE CHARACTER TRIANGLE

Every character is built of a complex combination of qualities. Some characters are funny, others are serious. Some are free-spirited and adventurous; some are careful and quiet. Some are kind. Some are... not kind. Some are open and others are closed off. Some come from dark, troubled backgrounds and others have histories of ease and privilege. You can attribute so many qualities to any one character that it almost seems like there are too many choices to make, too many directions you can go in. The Character Triangle helps you to think about these qualities, and balance them in a way that creates strong, vibrant, and compelling characters.

STRENGTHS. WEAKNESSES. VULNERABILITY.

The first thing you want to do is think about character building in three categories: strengths, weaknesses, and vulnerability. Strengths and weaknesses refer to qualities your character possesses; vulnerability is the thing that your character wishes to be rid of.

STRENGTHS:
The things a character can capably do

Strengths are where your character is on their game. These are the qualities a character has that make readers respect them. These are the capabilities and competencies that this character will rely upon to get them out of the water when it gets hot.

Strengths are characteristics we generally respect, like intelligence, kindness, and charisma.

WEAKNESSES:
The things a character can't capably do

Weaknesses are where your character falters, where they are less competent and capable. Weaknesses clue us in to a character's range of imperfection; imperfection is part of being human. A character's weaknesses may throw them right back into the hot water a strength just got them out of.

Weaknesses sound like bad qualities, but they are not. A perfect character is like Teflon; nothing sticks to it. Perfection is not believable or interesting, and for your character to be accessible at all to your reader, they must be believable.

Weaknesses can be harmless or even endearing characteristics, like social awkwardness, clumsiness, or the inability to tell a joke properly.

VULNERABILITY:
The source of your character's emotional pain

Vulnerability is a big topic, and it's the least intuitive because vulnerability sucks and we don't like to talk about it or think about it.

I mean… right? Think about your deepest vulnerability, the thing that any time you get near it, your heart rate quickens and your eyes start to tear up and your throat tightens.

Yeah. I'm talking about *that* thing.

That's not something you pull out at parties or when you've just met your significant others' boss. You don't pull that one out *ever*. Maybe not even *with* your significant other. But the thing is, in order to have true connection with another person, we need to share at least some vulnerability. It's the part of each of us that allows us to recognize each other as human.

Here's an exercise. I want you to imagine a person who appears practically perfect in every way. They're always impeccably dressed, they drive a beautiful car, they have a big fancy house, their kids are always well-behaved. They have loads of friends. They're not even mean, so you can't hate them and feel justified. They're just… perfect.

Ugh.

Are you at all interested in that person? I mean… at *all*?

Probably not. But imagine that you bump into that person in the grocery store and you make eye contact and you *have* to smile and say hello because you're not a jerk, so you say hello, and before they can even respond, they start crying. Not that perfect little track of one tear that doesn't even muss the mascara. I mean... *ugly* crying. Sobbing like they're gonna break in half. Mascara *everywhere*.

Ah... right there. Did you feel that? You don't even know why they are crying, but your heart just went, *Oh, baby*. You had no interest in this person a minute ago, but now, your empathy is engaged, and *you don't even know why they're crying*.

That's connection, and that's what vulnerability does, in fiction just like in real life because fiction *is* real to readers. That means that, in order for readers to connect emotionally to a character, they need the same thing we all need to feel connected to each other; vulnerability.

Brené Brown's work on vulnerability really opened this up for me. I watched her TED Talk and heard her say this: "In order for connection to happen, we have to allow ourselves to be seen, really seen."

Well, *that* hit me in the face. I mean, not just personally... although, yes, also that... but professionally. I realized then that the element of character building I'd been struggling with was in that talk. It wasn't just understanding what vulnerability was; I'd had a sense of that. It was that in order to feel connected, we have to *share* vulnerability.

In real life, total ugh. In fiction? Jackpot, baby.

But here's what you need to know about vulnerability; a little goes a long way. In your character triangle, you might have a great number of strengths and weaknesses, but you only need one solid vulnerability to make a character feel real. For a protagonist or an antagonist, you may want to amp up the pain presented in that vulnerability; for a supporting character, you can go a little lighter.

By the way, you're gonna hate me for this, but the best way to think about vulnerability in characters is to get comfortable with your own vulnerability and that of others. For that work, I recommend Brené Brown's *Rising Strong*; Glennon Doyle's podcast "We Can Do Hard

Things;" Elizabeth Gilbert's *Eat, Pray, Love;* and Cheryl Strayed's *Tiny Beautiful Things.*

While you're doing that work—which will be the work of the rest of your life, you are welcome and I am sorry—let me give you a few shortcuts to help you think about vulnerability in your characters.

WELLS OF VULNERABILITY

There are four "wells" of vulnerability that are good places to start as you try to think about how to build your characters with vulnerability. They are **fear, identity, love,** and **shame**. Like PGAG and ASPA, there is a useful acronym to help you remember the wells of vulnerability: FILS.

FILS:
Fear
Identity
Love
Shame

There are more sources of vulnerability than you can reasonably count, but drawing from any one of these four wells can give you a strong starting place for building your character's specific expression of vulnerability if you're not sure where to start.

Here are some examples of vulnerabilities that can come from these wells.

Fear: A character is so afraid of seeing her ex that she can't leave her house.

Identity: A nun decides she no longer believes in God.

Love: A salesman is deeply in love with the office receptionist, but she's already engaged to a guy in the warehouse.

Shame: A young actress goes to her first big Hollywood premiere and ends up on the worst-dressed list, where the entertainment writer also mocks her Appalachian accent.

VULNERABILITY VS. WEAKNESS

A question I am often asked when talking about the character triangle is the difference between vulnerabilities and weaknesses, and that can be confusing, so let's get to the core of that difference.

A weakness is something the character is not good at, but it's not necessarily a source of pain.

For example, I have a terrible sense of direction. Every now and again, I turn my phone's GPS on and it tells me to head west and I laugh and say, "You're kidding, right?" Like I know where "west" is. I'm not proud of it; I've gotten lost inside a mall.

While staring at the mall map.

But this isn't a source of pain for me. I think it's funny. If someone laughed at me and said, "Ha ha, you got lost in a mall," I'd laugh right along with them and then tell them about the time I got lost in a convenience store.

In a story, a weakness like a bad sense of direction can be narratively valuable; a character gets lost, and it leads to misadventure. But if it's not also a deep source of pain, then it's not vulnerability. It's just a weakness.

On the other hand, if a character's identity is tied to being a park ranger and a solid sense of direction is central to that identity, then the weakness of having a bad sense of direction could be a source of shame or pain. The character might try to hide that weakness from others, because if their boss found out, they could lose their job. In that case, a bad sense of direction *would* be a vulnerability.

A bad sense of direction can be either a weakness or a vulnerability; the distinction is whether or not it is a source of pain.

VULNERABILITY VS. VULNERABILITIES

I stated earlier in this chapter that a character can have a long list of both strengths and weaknesses, but they only need one vulnerability. Let's talk about that a bit more.

Have you ever had a friend who was always in the shit? Every day, something terrible or tragic is happening; every day, they are laying their pain at your feet, and every day, it's a new source of pain.

Your friend may just be having a string of bad luck; we've all had that. But when this is constant, when the bad run never passes, you are speared on the sharp end of weaponized vulnerability. When vulnerability isn't real, it's being used to elicit empathy and/or avoid personal responsibility. Who is going to criticize them when they're already so pathetic? What kind of cruel monster would dare expect them to take personal responsibility when they're in this state? That's not real vulnerability and eventually, we learn to see it for what it is: manipulation. At that point, we disengage because this person with whom we've deeply connected has just shown us that the vulnerability they've shared isn't real, and that is a betrayal.

The same thing can happen when a character has too many vulnerabilities; it reads as dishonest, and if we don't trust your character, we cannot emotionally connect with them.

Another response to too many vulnerabilities is emotional exhaustion, especially for readers who are empaths, who actually feel the pain of others. Fictional characters, remember, read as real to us in our response to them. We love them and we hate them the way we do real people; sometimes, even more so. When a character is just a mess of vulnerability walking around, they can trigger an overload response, which will prevent your reader from connecting to that character.

And the last reason not to overload on vulnerability is that your story gets stronger when you can tie a protagonist's vulnerability to their goal, and thus, to the central narrative conflict. If you have a lot of vulnerabilities, you weaken that connection.

My advice: Pick one strong vulnerability and stick with it.

WRITING VULNERABILITY

We've learned a couple of things about vulnerability. It's how people connect.

And no one wants to talk about theirs. Most of the time, no one wants to even think about theirs.

With that being the case, how can you write about vulnerability and make it seem genuine?

Good question, and the answer lies in the skilled use of **negative space**.

Let's go to the example I used earlier of a love-based vulnerability with our salesman who is in love with the office receptionist who is engaged to a guy who works in the warehouse. Intrepid readers will have identified this example as inspired by the American version of the sitcom *The Office*. If you watch the pilot episode, you see that Jim never tells us that he's in love with Pam. In fact, we won't hear him admit that for some time. But we know immediately. How?

First, we see that Jim and Pam have fun together at the office, as he is often at the front desk laughing with her.

Later, we see an interview where Jim mentions Pam's favorite flavor of yogurt. In Pam's interview, she blushes and looks away when she learns that he guessed correctly.

Toward the end of that episode, Pam's fiancé Roy shows up to take her home after work. Jim is barely able to look at Roy; he hangs his head while the two men stand at the front desk awkwardly waiting for Pam to return from doing her last task before going home.

Then, in another interview, we see Jim repeat a question asked of him by the documentary crew; does he think he will be invited to the wedding?

He doesn't answer.

That's negative space.

One of the best ways to draw your reader in is to give them negative space in which to intuit what is happening based on what is *not* being textually said or acknowledged. You hint at vulnerability by pushing your character toward something and then watching them actively walk around it. The space your character avoids gives us a big clue as to where their vulnerability is; I call those clues **vulnerability markers**.

VULNERABILITY MARKER:
The negative space a character leaves around their vulnerability to avoid addressing the source of their emotional pain

Vulnerability markers are important. Even if you're writing a first-person novel, which is deeply intimate, sometimes the character isn't aware of or being honest with themselves about their vulnerabilities, so even in the most intimate of media, readers need vulnerability markers to show us where the treasure is hidden.

For Jim, the vulnerability marker is in what he doesn't say about being invited to a wedding. A character who changes the subject whenever anyone talks about, say, their sister, is laying down a huge vulnerability marker; something is going on with regard to that sister. As readers, we are trained to recognize vulnerability markers. As writing devices, they are powerful because they require the reader to lean in and intuit what is happening, which makes the experience more believable. I'm more inclined to believe what I figure out on my own than what I've been told. Plus, when a reader's intuition is later confirmed, they get a little hit of dopamine from guessing correctly. Your story gave them a treat, so they're going to be more engaged, in case more treats are waiting.

STRENGTHS AND WEAKNESSES

I went in deep with vulnerability because that is probably the most challenging and least intuitive concept in the character triangle; let's circle back around and spend a little more time on the two other vertices of the triangle: strengths and weaknesses.

These are pretty straightforward. Strengths are things your character is good at. Weaknesses are things your character is not good at. Strengths make us respect and like your character; weaknesses make your character human and relatable.

But a virtue, taken to an extreme, can become a vice.

A detective's intellect could be a strength, and we may be amazed at how he can deduce who a murderer is from a stray dog hair found on the victim's shoe. But that same intellect may be wielded to keep people at bay, and it could prevent him from making meaningful human connections. His intellect might dull his compassion; he might, in fact, rely on it so much that he's kind of an asshole.

In that case, his intellect is both a strength and a weakness.

Or what about when a weakness becomes a strength? A rural hobbit's extreme simplicity seems like it would compromise the very important task of saving his world from an evil presence that sows darkness in the hearts of men. Later, however, it's that very simplicity that allows him to resist the pull of that darkness and carry his friend on his back in the final push to destroy that evil.

In this example, what seems like a weakness becomes a strength.

Another thing to consider when working with the character triangle is that you don't need to balance out strengths and weaknesses. A character who is mostly weaknesses and few strengths is ripe for a hell of a character arc (the transformation a character shows over the course of a story). A character who is mostly strengths and few weaknesses is ripe for a wicked fall from grace. Those are both fun playgrounds for any writer.

THE LIKEABILITY MYTH

Before we finish up with character, I want to hit on the likeability myth, because while it's a myth, it illustrates beautifully how powerful the character triangle is.

Most writers who have written anything that they've let anyone else read has probably been told that a character isn't likeable enough. This especially happens when a character is a woman because of societal expectations that women need to be "nice." Please allow me to destroy the likeability myth right now.

Sherlock Holmes. Walter White. Annalise Keating. Tony Soprano. Gregory House. Tyrion Lannister. Spike from *Buffy the Vampire Slayer;* Red from *Orange is the New Black*. One thing that all these characters have in common is that they're not always terribly likeable. They're not good people doing good things, but they're great characters. These and many more characters through the ages are textual proof that likeability is not a requirement for any character, protagonist or otherwise.

All that said, when you get the likeability feedback, don't ignore it. "Likeability" is common shorthand for a real problem; your reader is having trouble connecting with your character. Characters don't need to be likeable; they need to be compelling. And what makes them compelling?

A solid mix of strengths, weaknesses, and vulnerability.

BALANCING THE CHARACTER TRIANGLE

Capital-G Good characters are hellishly boring. A white hat who is so perfect and good that they will never do bad things, they will never fail, they will never make a mistake, they will never have true vulnerability… *blech*, amirite? A character like this has no place to go, nothing to learn. All strengths and no weaknesses make Jack a very, very dull character.

In addition, all weaknesses and no strengths… well, it's a little better but it can also be uncomfortable and exhausting after a while. A little bit of Gollum goes a long way.

But when you get your balance right by ensuring that each character has at least some qualities from each vertex of the character triangle, you build a compelling character.

Let's take Walter White from *Breaking Bad*. At first glance, he seems like a character who is almost all weakness and vulnerability, and very little strength. He's kind of mousy; he doesn't stand up for himself. His weakness is being literally weak. He's also very sick with cancer; being faced with death is a huge vulnerability, especially because he doesn't make enough money to afford the treatment, and he's going to leave his pregnant wife and disabled son with nothing when he dies.

Walter does have some strengths, though; he's very smart, and has a deep knowledge of chemistry. This allows him to start cooking and dealing meth, and it turns out he's *really* good at being a drug dealer. As the story moves forward, he gets better and better at a very bad thing, and he likes it. We start to see what happens, not when a good man goes bad, but when a weak man is tempted. The strength that Walter develops is corrupted by his overall moral weakness.

Does this sound like a likeable character? Not really. But compelling? Hell yeah.

And note, we don't need an *equal* mix of strengths, weaknesses and vulnerability; we need the *right* mix.

THE CHARACTER TOOLBOX

The character triangle is probably the biggest character-building tool in your toolbox, but there are other things that can help breathe life into your characters and make them real to you, which will make them real to your readers.

PLACEHOLDERS

One of the most powerful tools for me is using placeholders. These are real people that you base your character on. Does that feel to you like cheating? Get over it. It's not. Placeholders are a starting point for your character, but before long, your characters become their own people and leave their placeholders behind. Again, you're taking inspiration, not plagiarizing. You can base a character on Snow White or Angela Merkel or your favorite teacher from elementary school or Tom Hanks or whoever inspires you. This helps with making a character feel real because you're using the affectations and quirks of a real person to help bring flavor to your dialogue and action descriptions, and that helps that character become real to you a little faster. Once the character is real to you, they often shed their placeholders and honestly, I've forgotten most of my character's original placeholders.

The other nice thing about placeholders is that they are great for collaging. If you're using Robert Downey, Jr. as a placeholder for a character, you can do a Google search and find pictures of the actor that feel like your character. You can save those to a file on your computer and print them out for a physical collage or put them into a digital collage with Photoshop or Canva, or just save the links to a private Pinterest board where you keep images that inspire your story. It works like a charm; give it a try.

NAME BIBLE

If you have a story with a Jim, a John, a Jennifer, a Jackie, and a Josie, it can be hard for your reader to keep track, especially in a novel. A handy strategy for avoiding this problem is creating a character name bible. This is a simple document—spreadsheets work well here—with a line for each letter of the alphabet. Every time you name a character, you put that name next to the letter. When you see yourself with a handful of characters with the same first letter, switch it up. I have found in the past that, for some reason, I am mostly like to use M or J names. I have no idea why. But using a name bible keeps me from overdoing it on any one letter and forces me into a more thoughtful and conscious state when naming characters.

You never want to name a character casually. Always work to find the right name.

Another thing you want to avoid is a repetitive sound. I love names that have an -*ee* sound at the end. Jamie, Maggie, Jenny, Daisy, Sherry. That kind of thing can get old after a while in film and television where we are hearing the names, but it can also be a problem for text readers. Many people subvocalize when reading text, which means they perform the word in their head while reading, so how a name sounds is important even in a text-based form.

A handy strategy for getting great names is using a baby naming website. Go and scan through what's there, find what appeals to you. You'll see names you wouldn't think of right away, that have flavor and style to them. You can search for names by family descent; maybe your character comes from an Irish or Iranian family. That can help you find interesting, less common names.

TROPES

We're going to veer away from character for just a moment, because what I'm about to say applies to all aspects of storytelling, but we'll land back on character, so just hang on for a minute while we go off road.

TROPE:
A repeated storytelling device or element

Tropes are defined differently in different spaces; for our purposes here at *How Story Works*, we're including not just repeated story elements—such as the damsel in distress or the love triangle—but writing devices as well, such as flashback, voice over, and prologue.

Tropes are often referenced with an accompanying eye-roll or sneer, simply because their repetitive nature hits the originality panic button, but it's important to remember that tropes are value neutral. They are, of themselves, neither good nor bad. The fact that they repeat is a feature, not a bug; their repetition charges their power. Right now, relieve yourself of any negative associations with tropes, because when they are used with thoughtful purpose, they can be a writer's best friend.

But to help you accept this as true facts, let's take a moment to talk about originality.

THE ORIGINALITY FALLACY

One of the most counter-productive mindsets I've seen in writers is the idea that originality is a primary value to storytelling. It's not true; originality has very limited value in storytelling.

Let me repeat, for those in the back; originality has very limited value in storytelling.

Now, I'm not saying that as blanket permission to go out and plagiarize to your heart's content; don't slippery slope me, I will not play that game. What I mean is that *every* story has been told, every writing device has been used, every scenario has been played out, every character has been written.

There is no such thing as an original story.

And also, *every* story is original. We'll crack that nut in a minute; stick with me here.

In recent years, I have noticed that my students will often prioritize the twist, shocking reveal or surprise ending over the rest of their storytelling. They twist their stories into pretzels and then add scaffolding to hold the pretzel up, all to accommodate a surprise that often wasn't worth all that was sacrificed to uphold it. The irony is that most of the time the scaffolding is so obvious that the reader can see the "shocking surprise" coming a mile away.

Am I going to argue that there's no real pleasure to be had in a genuine surprise? Absolutely not. When well executed, a twist can be loads of fun. It's just that writers will often treat the "twist" like a primary value, as if the main job of a story is to be something we haven't seen before. Okay, sure, it's fun to have a twist that recontextualizes a story, and when you read it a second time knowing what's coming, it's like reading a whole new story from a different perspective. Season one of the NBC comedy *The Good Place* is a great example of this.

I'm not gonna spoil that; go watch and you'll see what I'm talking about.

But my point is, *yes*, there is a very particular pleasure that comes from a well-orchestrated twist, and if you can pull that off—more power to you. But know this; your story doesn't *need* that to be a good story. There are many, many more values to storytelling than a shocking surprise, and in general, writers are sacrificing way too much to achieve an end that is... you know... *okay*, but not the end-all, be-all of storytelling.

Here's proof: Do you have a book or movie that you love and you engage with over and over and over again? If the surprise and the twist were the only narrative values of any worth, then why would you do that? You already know what happens. Why are you engaging with it again?

Because storytelling is about *so much more than surprise*. There are a million different pleasures that come from engaging with story. A good twist is only one of them, and it's not even in the top ten. A writer obsessed with chasing originality is a writer who is wasting much of their time and energy because...

... and here's where *my* twist comes in...

... you can't *help* but be original.

The story you're telling may have been told a million times before, but this is the first time *you* are telling it. And because you are the only you anywhere in existence, the story you tell, even when it shares elements with stories that have been told over and over for millennia, will be original because you are you and you honestly couldn't *not* be original if you tried.

Sure, vampire stories have been told before, but not by you. Do you think *Buffy the Vampire Slayer* and *True Blood* are interchangeable? Both story worlds have vampires, as did *Dracula* and *The Vampire Diaries* and *Interview with a Vampire*. But they're told by completely different people, who created completely different worlds.

Here's an exercise: Sit five writers down and tell them to tell the story of Cinderella, and force them to include the following elements in their story: Cinderella's mother died; her father remarried; she has a stepmother and two stepsisters who are spoiled while she has to do all the housework; she wants to go to the ball; the steps make it impossible for her to go to the ball; her fairy godmother shows up and makes with the magic; she goes to the ball and meets the prince, who falls in love with her; she runs away at midnight when her magic spell will fade; the prince hunts for her; the stepmother and stepsisters try to block her; and the prince finds her anyway and marries her.

Everything else, they can do whatever they want. You know what will happen? You will get five vastly different versions of this same old story. One might take place in a war-torn London in the 40s; the other might take place in a futuristic Ghana. One might focus on

Cinderella; another might have the stepmother or a stepsister as the protagonist.

There are a million ways to tell the same story. Your stories will always be original, as long as you make your highest primary value be *you*; your perspective, your voice, your view of the world.

Your *magic*, if you will.

It's important to have the originality talk as we get into tropes because there are writers out there who bristle at the idea of doing anything that has been done before, and that belief is inherently limiting.

Some tropes are destructive, sure. Stereotypes absolutely are. But archetypes are not. And many tropes—from writing devices like prologues, to story beats like chase scenes, to conflict structures like a love triangle—are returned to by writers because there is something of value in those elements.

Speaking of archetypes, here's where we veer back into character.

ARCHETYPE:
A character whose defining characteristics relate to their role in the story

This character is who they are because of the role they play in the narrative, which exists independently of race, gender or any other character quality. The mentor; the trickster; the maid, mother, and crone. Archetypes are repeated across a number of stories but are expressed in new ways and brought into new contexts. Because their defining purpose is attached to their role, archetypes are helpful to building deep and meaningful narratives.

STEREOTYPE:
A character whose defining characteristics relate to one identity they hold

Stereotypes exist at a shallow, surface level; a stereotype is a package of characteristics that are automatically assigned based on one identity. A character is female; therefore she must love to shop and be a terrible driver. A character is Asian; therefore, they must be good at math. A character is gay; therefore he is flashy and flamboyant and promiscuous.

Stereotypes make a character less human by forcing them into the realm of caricature; that is the opposite of what you want to do with your characters.

BUILDING CHARACTERS WITH ARCHETYPES

Archetypes are incredibly valuable because they are based on the role a character plays in the story, so they can help you with building character, conflict, and structure. There are tons of archetypes out there, and once you start researching, you're going to see them everywhere. *Oh, there's a trickster! There's a mentor!* That kind of thing.

Your friends are going to be *really* annoyed.

Let's start with the archetypes you have seen so often that you might not have realized they are archetypes: the hero and the villain.

As we discussed in the chapter on conflict, the hero and the villain do not automatically map to protagonist and antagonist. But hero and villain are archetypes because they are about the role they play in the story; one is the representative from Right, and the other the delegate from Wrong.

Here are some other archetypes to think about.

THE MENTOR

The **mentor** is the experienced, usually older, character who trains the young newbie and makes them ready to be a hero. The mentor also often dies in the course of the story, which forces the new young upstart to come out and do their thing on their own, fully in their own power.

Fun fact: We first got the mentor archetype from the character named Mentor in Homer's *The Iliad* and *The Odyssey*; he was an old guy who gave advice.

Examples of the mentor archetype in modern stories are: Gandalf from *The Lord of the Rings*; Obi-Wan Kenobi from *Star Wars*; Mr. Miyagi from *The Karate Kid*; Miranda Priestly from *The Devil Wears Prada* (not all mentors are nice about it); Jean Milburn in *Sex Education*; Patches O'Houlihan in *Dodgeball*.

THE TRICKSTER

The Trickster is often a shapeshifter, either literally or metaphorically. They are the character who's smarter than everyone else, who can always find a way to get themselves out of scrapes by using everyone else's stupidity or vanity against them. In African mythology, we have Anansi, or Spider; the Hopi have Kokopelli. Loki came from Norse mythology.

Examples of this kind of character in modern stories are Loki from the Marvel Cinematic Universe; the Joker from *Batman*; Susan in *Bringing Up Baby*; Root on *Person of Interest*; the roadrunner from the Warner Brothers cartoons; The Doctor from *Doctor Who*.

THE THREE

The Three (also known as the maid, mother and crone; the three witches; the triple goddess; the graces; the furies; the seasons; the fates) is a group archetype that gives us three (typically female, but not necessarily so) characters with aspects of generational separation, although they don't need to literally be from different generations. The maid is the innocent child; the mother is the responsible adult; and the crone is the wise person who is often quirky and unpredictable. We see them expressed all over the place in mythology and folklore around the world, with so many different names and identities that they are almost also shapeshifters and tricksters as well.

In modern stories, you see the maid, mother, and crone in Magrat, Nanny Ogg and Granny Weatherwax in Terry Pratchett's *Discworld* novels; Rory, Lorelai, and Emily in the *Gilmore Girls*; Abby, Daisy and Shar in *Dogs and Goddesses*; and they appear as "The Three" under almost all the names in Neil Gaiman's *Sandman* comic book series, although I enjoy when they go by Cynthia, Mordred, and Mildred.

Those are just a few examples of tropes and archetypes; I recommend doing some research and keeping a notebook of your favorites. When you need them for a story, you'll have a resource ready to pull from.

THE MOST IMPORTANT THING TO REMEMBER

We've discussed a lot of things in this chapter on character, but if you only remember one thing, let it be this:

Characters are not characters.

They are people.

To your readers, they are real people. Flesh and blood. They are people we love and care for; hate and take vengeance upon; fear and retreat from; miss and mourn. Think about the triangle, use the tropes to help you create, but at some point in your writing, these characters will become people and when they do, don't be afraid to let *them* lead *you*.

8. ON MEANING

We've spent this time together talking about how to build effective stories, and you now have what you need to do that, but before I let you go, I want to spend a little time asking ourselves one question.

Why?

Why do we tell stories? Why do we want to? Why does storytelling (a.k.a., the entertainment industry) rake in almost all of our disposable income? Movies, plays, books, television, video games... we're insatiable.

Why?

It's a worthwhile question. And I'm pretty sure I have the answer.

Meaning.

As we discussed at the start of this book, the *why* is everything. When things change and we assign a *why* to that change, we create meaning. We create and tell stories to provide ourselves with a constant stream of the one resource that humans generate and cannot live without: Meaning.

Why do we take characters and put them through hell? Why do we force them into uncomfortable situations where they have to make impossible choices in order to maybe win in a battle that is life or death to them?

Because when we force a character to change, we create meaning.

How that character changes, how their world changes, gives us *meaning*.

Stories are entertaining and educational and experiential, but at the end of the day, they are machines that generate meaning, and that is what we go to them for. Stories generate meaning by creating a world and then changing it, and we derive meaning by examining the differences between the old world and the new, and deciding what that means.

If the story is one of hope, then what was learned or achieved within the story will make the world better. Good vanquishes evil, and everything is sunny and bright and safe.

If it's a darker story, maybe good doesn't so much vanquish evil as set it back a bit, but you know that whatever spot of light was won in this fight, it's not a permanent victory.

If it's a tragedy, darkness wins.

The classic version of Little Red Riding Hood ends with Red and Granny just fine—if you ignore the almost-certain battle with post-traumatic stress that will be coming for both of them—and the woodsman is the hero of the day, having saved them both.

But remember what we said way back at the beginning? That the storyteller doesn't decide what a story means, the reader does?

Well… let's take a moment and *read* how the world has changed from the start of that version (women who leave the safety of home are in danger from men with ill-intent) to the end (women are safe because a man was in the right place at the right time).

Did my read give you a little twinge of discomfort? There's good reason for that if it did. This is a story most of us, in western culture at least, have been fed since we were little, way before we had the cognitive ability to fight back, to think critically about the implicit messaging… or meaning… we were being given through the IV drip of story.

But do I lie? Young Red is in danger from the wolf, who is coded male. She remains in danger until another character, textually male, saves her.

During the entire story, neither woman—Red nor Granny—has any agency of her own. They are helpless victims, waiting on one man to kill them, another to save them.

Little Red Riding Hood is a tale of the patriarchy both threatening and saving women at the same time. Man is both beast and savior, tormenter and rescuer, feeding the poison and then delivering the cure, over and over and over again. He is always central, no matter what role he plays. If Red had been smarter… if she hadn't told the Wolf where Granny's house was… if she hadn't looked so delicious… if she hadn't strayed from the path… if she hadn't gone into the damn woods to begin with, none of it would have happened, so really…

…if you think about it…

…it's all *her* fault.[14]

Okay. *Wow.* So, am I saying that our stories have been feeding women belief systems of victimhood and disempowerment for centuries so that our culture could groom them for abuse and subjugation?

I mean… yeah. That's kind of exactly what I'm saying, and it's not just women. The stories we have told have been in turns imprisoning and liberating us all in a constant cycle since the dawn of time.

---

[14] Just so we're clear… it's super fucking not.

The point that I'm making here is not that our collective cultural psyche has taken on a lot of water due to the stories we've told and how we've told them, although that is definitely true, but that a story may seem simple, its component parts mechanical, its surface-level message childish even, and still, it can have the power to shape the way people experience themselves and the world around them for centuries.

In a quote commonly attributed to Plato, but for which I cannot find a proper citation, "Those who tell the stories rule society." And it makes sense; if humans are desperately and constantly in search of meaning, if we are perpetually on the hunt for the why, then the person who provides that meaning, who gives us the why… well, that person is running the whole game.

Stories are fun and entertaining and delightful and scary and thrilling and sad, but they are also *power*, and never in the history of our world has that power been so democratized. You wanna take that power back? You do that by understanding how stories work, and using the power you wield with them consciously and purposefully. Yes, you can entertain and educate and provide experience, but while you do that, you can generate meaning and build narratives that empower and heal as well.

You can rewrite Little Red Riding Hood to be anything you want.

You can give Red a little more agency. A little less fear.

You can use an internal conflict in a girl who wants to be a woman, but who knows that transformation will cost her something, even if she doesn't yet know what.

You can make Wolf a character who gets consent, and still destroys.

You can finish the story in a nuanced place where darkness and light dance together, and are not entirely unhappy with the arrangement.

You can change the world.

ACKNOWLEDGEMENTS

My work, outlined in this book, is the cumulation of what I've learned from others, and what I've discovered on my own working from the knowledge they gave me.

My deepest gratitude goes to:

Denise Gardner, my favorite teacher in high school, who was one of the first people to tell me I should be a writer.

Professor Peter Moller, who told me I should be a writer in college.

Chris Baty, who founded Nanowrimo and gave me the absolute most valuable piece of writing advice I've ever received: Write crap.

Jessica Page Morrell, for her iVillage classes in the early aughts. She thought I was good, and that had never really occurred to me before. She also connected me with her agent, who is now my agent.

Stephanie Kip Rostan, that agent, who has been a cheerleader and supporter even when I didn't make her any money.

Dr. Kelly Jones, who I like to call my pedagogical midwife, who has used her expertise in learning to help me transform my knowledge into something students can absorb, understand and apply. If anything I say here makes any sense at all, you can thank Dr. Jones.

The people who have studied story with me, challenging me when I needed it so that I could back up my arguments: Dr. Kelly Jones, Noelle LaCroix, Alisa Kwitney, Joshua Unruh, Rob Heiret, C.J.

Barry, Anne Stuart, Jennifer Crusie, and all the listeners on social media who called me out and in as necessary.

My students, who took this theory and jumped up and down on it like the monkeys in that old American Tourister commercial. I appreciate the irony that they're all way too young to understand that reference.

Michael Schoonmaker, who has been the person to hire me whenever I needed hiring, and who gave me college classrooms in which to teach.

Vaughn Schoonmaker, one of my first students, now a dear friend who teaches my theory in his classes.

Ian Martin, whose love and support and patience and humor made the grueling process of writing non-fiction almost fun.

Thank you all.

Author's Note

Hello, reader!

Traditional publishing gives me the heaves, for a lot of reasons, but mostly because you're signing all of your rights away for about 8% of the profits, and you still have to do all of your own marketing, which is my least favorite part of this gig. Still, I tried to sell this book traditionally, just in case I could get what it was worth. The idea of getting paid for my work up front was too good to resist.

I didn't get a single offer.

Now, don't cry for me, Argentina. I get it. I'm terrible at self-promotion, and despite the fact that this book is… I believe… stone-cold genius, I don't at the time of this writing have a big enough platform to entice a book industry that has stopped taking risks. You know how many people are trying to sell writing books? Loads. You know how many have bigger platforms than I do?

Like… *all* of 'em.

I'm not going to say I breathed a sigh of relief when all of New York City rejected me, that never feels great, but I understood why. They liked the book, they said, but they'd have to work too hard to sell it in an already crowded market. I didn't weep into my Cream of Wheat for too long; there are huge benefits to independent publishing. I have all the skills I need to do it on my own, I have total artistic control, and I get 100% of the profits. That doesn't suck.

That said, I'm going to ask you for a favor. As I said, I suck at self-promotion. I'm going to work on it, I have major plans for 2022 when this book comes out, and hopefully they include visiting a town near you, but if you found this book helpful, if you think it's as good as I think it is, I want to ask you now to tell two people about it. That's it. Just two people.

However, if you *really* like this book, you can do more. You can shout about it on social media, with a link to the Amazon page. Write a review on Amazon, Goodreads, your favorite bathroom wall, wherever you like. Bring it to your writing groups. Have your writing group reach out to me at lanidianerich.com and invite me to speak.

I need your help. I have a lot of strengths, but self-promotion is not one of them. I believe in this book, though, so I'm going to try to get past that.

Thank god it's only a weakness and not a vulnerability, am I right?

And thank *you* for taking the time to get all the way to the end and see this note. I appreciate any help you can give me with this. Maybe between us, we'll be able to make some waves.

Everything,

L

P.S. If you're wondering why I sign my letters with "everything, L" then you should sign up for my newsletter at:

dearwriter.substack.com.

P.P.S. Did you see me just promote myself? Darling, *that's* a character arc.

GLOSSARY

act: a sequence of scenes which work together to alter the relationship of the protagonist to the central narrative conflict, bringing on a new approach toward or perspective on that conflict

anchor scene: a scene which significantly and purposefully escalates the central narrative conflict

antagonist: the character whose goal blocks the protagonist's goal

archetype: a character whose defining characteristics relate to their role in the story

ASPA: (formula for strong goals) Active; Specific; Personal; Achievable

beat: a single unit of narrative change

central narrative conflict: a goal-based conflict upon which the structure of a story is built

character: a fictional representation of a person

coding: when a thing is textually one thing, but meaningfully or representationally another

composition: a narrative unit that launches, escalates, and resolves a central narrative conflict and then shows how the world has changed

conflict: a struggle between two opposing forces; also, the fuel that keeps your story moving

craft: the set of principles that guide storytelling

event: a moment of change

external conflict: a conflict between a protagonist and something external to themselves

false conflict: any conflict that would be immediately dissolved if the parties involved have an honest conversation

FILS: (wells of vulnerability) Fear; Identity; Love; Shame

form: the medium through which an artist works.

goal: an event a character wants to bring about

hero: (trope; archetype) a character in a story aligned with goodness

internal conflict: a conflict between a protagonist and themselves; a conflict when a protagonist wants two things that are mutually exclusive

magic: the artistic imprint of a creator on their work

meaning: the implied or explicit significance of a thing

mundane conflict: conflict that is based on philosophical or personal differences; conflict not based on goals

narrative: the meaning evoked by a story

narrative conflict: a goal-based conflict between a protagonist with a goal and an antagonist with a mutually exclusive goal

narrative structure: a structure sequenced purposefully to evoke a unified meaning or significance

narrative transport: when a reader's current reality fades away, and the reader lives for a time within the reality of the story

narrative units: an expression of events within a story

negative goal: an eventuality the protagonist wishes to avoid

parallel narrative: a completely separate, but equally prevalent, storyline with its own escalating central narrative conflict

PGAG: (formula for central narrative conflict) Protagonist/Goal vs. Antagonist/Goal

positive goal: an eventuality the protagonist wishes to happen

protagonist: the character whose perspective directs the reader's experience of a story

reader: any person who derives meaning from any story, regardless of form

scene: a sequence of chronologically continuous beats, culminating in a larger narrative change

SEE Change: (formula for basic structure) Start the conflict; Escalate the conflict; End the conflict; Change the world

series: a sequence of compositions which work together to tell connected stories within a single world or thematic landscape

stereotype: a character whose defining characteristics relate to one identity they hold

story: a recounted event or series of events

storytelling: the art of building a story purposefully to serve a particular narrative

strengths: the things a character can capably do

structure: the order in which the events of a story are sequenced

subplot: a secondary, less prevalent storyline with its own escalating central narrative conflict.

supporting character: Every character that is not the protagonist nor the antagonist

trope: a repeated storytelling device or element

turning point: an anchor scene where the protagonist makes an active choice to escalate the central narrative conflict

villain: (trope; archetype) a character in a story aligned with evil

vulnerability: The source of your character's emotional pain

vulnerability marker: the negative space a character leaves around their vulnerability to avoid addressing the source of their emotional pain

weaknesses: The things a character can't capably do

EXERCISES & WORKSHEETS

Scan the following code to download the worksheet packet that accompanies this book, or visit bit.ly/hsw-worksheet.

BIBLIOGRAPHY

Aristotle. 2018. *Poetics (Norton Critical Editions)*. Edited by David Gorman and Michelle Zerba. New York, London: W. W. Norton & Company.

Atwood, Margaret. 1986. *The Handmaid's Tale*. New York: Houghton Mifflin Harcourt Publishing Co.

Batman. 1989. Directed by Tim Burton. Written by Bob Kane, Sam Hamm, & Warren Skaaren.

Baum, L Frank. 1900. *The Wonderful Wizard of Oz*. Chicago: George M. Hill Company.

Breaking Bad. 2008-2013. Created by Vince Gilligan.

Bringing Up Baby. 1938. Directed by Howard Hawks. Written by Dudley Nichols & Hagar Wilde.

Brown, Brené. 2012. Daring Greatly: How the Courage to Be Vulnerable Transforms the Way We Live, Love, Parent, and Lead. New York: Penguin Random House.

Brown, Brené. 2015. *Rising Strong*. New York: Spiegel & Grau.

Brown, Brené. June 2010. "The Power of Vulnerability." Houston, TX: TEDxHouston. https://www.ted.com/talks/brene_brown_the_power_of_vulnerability

Buffy the Vampire Slayer. 1997. Created by Joss Whedon.

Campbell, Joseph. 1990. The Hero's Journey: Joseph Campbell on His Life and Work. Novato: New World Library.

Crusie, Jennifer, Anne Stuart, and Lani Diane Rich. 2009. *Dogs and Goddesses.* New York: St. Martin's Press.

Decker, Dan. 1998. Anatomy of a Screenplay: Writing the American Screenplay from Character Structure to Convergence. Chicago: The Screenwriters Group.

Doctor Who. 2005. Created by Russell T. Davis, Steven Moffat, & Sydney Newman.

Dodgeball: A True Underdog Story. 2004. Directed and written by Rawson Marshall Thurber.

Doyle, Glennon. 2021. *We Can Do Hard Things.* Podcast.

http://wecandohardthingspodcast.com

Dr. Horrible's Sing Along Blog. 2008. Created by Joss Whedon.

French Kiss. 1995. Directed by Lawrence Kasdan. Written by Adam Brooks.

Gaiman, Neil. 1989. *Sandman (comic series).* New York: DC Comics.

Gaiman, Neil. 2021. *The Art of Storytelling.* Masterclass. https://www.masterclass.com/classes/neil-gaiman-teaches-the-art-of-storytelling

Gilbert, Elizabeth. 2007. *Eat, Pray, Love.* New York: Riverhead Books.

Gilbert, Elizabeth. 2015. *Big Magic: Creative Living Beyond Fear.* New York: Riverhead Books.

Gilmore Girls. 2000. Created by Amy Sherman Palladino.

Guardians of the Galaxy. 2014. Directed by James Gunn. Written by James Gunn, Nicole Perlman, & Dan Abnett.

His Girl Friday. 1940. Directed by Howard Hawks. Written by Charles Lederer, Ben Hecht, & Charles MacArthur.

Homer. 1919. *The Odyssey.* London; New York: W. Heinemann; G.P. Putnam's Sons.

Homer. 1955. *Iliad.* London; New York: Dent; Dutton.

Indiana Jones and the Raiders of the Lost Ark. 1981. Directed by Steven Spielberg. Written by Lawrence Kasdan, George Lucas, & Philip Kaufman.

Jaws 4: The Revenge. 1987. Directed by Joseph Sargent. Written by Peter Benchley & Michael de Guzman.

Maguire, Gregory. 2007. *Wicked.* New York: Harper.

Martin, George R.R. 1996. *A Game of Thrones.* New York: Bantam Books.

Matrin, George R.R. 2011. *A Dance with Dragons.* New York: Bantam Books.

McKee, Robert. 1997. Story: Substance, Structure, Style, and the Principles of Screenwriting. New York: ReganBooks.

Megamind. 2010. Directed by Tom McGrath. Written by Alan Schoolcraft & Brent Simons.

Memento. 2000. Directed by Christopher Nolan. Written by Christopher Nolan, Jonathan Nolan.

Moonlighting. 1985-1989. Created by Glenn Gordon Caron.

Nietzsche, Friedrich. 2003. Beyond Good and Evil: Prelude to a Philosophy of the Future. (translated by Walter Kaufmann). New York: Vintage Books; Random House.

Person of Interest. 2011. Created by Jonathan Nolan.

Pratchett, Terry. 1983. The Colour of Magic. New York: Harper Collins.

Rashomon. 1950. Directed by Akira Kurosawa. Written by Ryûnosuke Akutagawa, Akira Kurosawa, & Shinobu Hashimoto.

Rowling, J. K. 2007. Harry Potter and the Deathly Hallows. New York: Scholastic.

Roxanne. 1987. Directed by Fred Schepisi. Written by Edmond Rostand & Steve Martin.

Sex Education. 2019. Created by Laurie Nunn.

Snow White and the Seven Dwarfs. 1937. Directed by William Cottrell, David Hand, & Wilfred Jackson. Written by Jacob Grimm, Wilhelm Grimm, & Ted Sears.

Snyder, Blake. 2005. Save the Cat! The Last Book on Screenwriting You'll Ever Need. Studio City: Michael Wiese Productions.

Star Wars: Episode IV - A New Hope. 1977. Directed by George Lucas. Written by George Lucas.

Strayed, Cheryl. 2012. Tiny Beautiful Things: Advice on Life and Love from Dear Sugar. New York: Vintage Books; Random House.

Strunk, Jr., William, & E. B. White. 1999. The Elements of Style (4th ed.). New York: Pearson Education.

Tangled. 2010. Directed by Nathan Greno & Byron Howard. Written by Dan Fogelman, Jacob Grimm, & Wilhelm Grimm.

The Fugitive. 1993. Directed by Andrew Davies. Written by Jeb Stuart, David Twohy, & Roy Huggins.

The Good Place. 2014. Created by Michael Schur.

The Karate Kid. 1984. Directed by John G. Avildson. Written by Robert Mark Kamen.

The Office. 2005. Created by Greg Daniels.

Tolkien, J.R.R. 1991. The Fellowship of the Ring. London: HarperCollins.

Toy Story. 1995. Directed by John Lasseter. Written by John Lasseter, Pete Docter, & Andrew Stanton.

Vogler, Christopher. 2007. The Writer's Journey: Mythical Structure for Writers (3rd ed.). Studio City: Michael Wiese Productions.

Weir, Andy. 2011. The Martian. New York: Random House.

Weisberger, Lauren. 2004. The Devil Wears Prada. New York: Penguin Random House.

Young Adult. 2011. Directed by Jason Reitman. Written by Diablo Cody.

Zak, Paul. 2013, December 7. "How Stories Change the Brain." *Greater Good Science Center.* The Greater Good Science Center at the University of California, Berkeley. https://greatergood.berkeley.edu/article/item/how_stories_change _brain